Navigating Through the Shadows of Emotional Immaturity: The Path to Healing from Parental Wounds

A Comprehensive Manual for Understanding, Confronting, and Growing Beyond the Complexities of Relationships with Emotionally Distant Parents.

Daniel Mendici

1. Definition of Emotionally Immature Parents:

- Explain who they are and what characteristics emotionally immature parents have.

2. Origins of Emotional Immaturity:

- Examine the historical, psychological, and cultural reasons behind emotional immaturity.

3. The Impact of Emotional Immaturity on Childhood:

- Analyze how children grow up in an environment with emotionally immature parents.

4. Signs and Symptoms in Children:

- Identify typical behaviors and signals of children living in these conditions.

5. Long-Term Consequences:

- Explore how these childhood issues influence adult life in terms of relationships, career, and overall well-being.

6. The Role of Money and Power:

- Analyze how emotional immaturity can influence economic and power-related decisions within the family.

7. Adaptation Strategies:

- Examine the tactics children adopt to cope, such as denial, isolation, or conformity.

8. Rediscovering the Self:

- Offer advice on how adults can reconnect with their true selves and passions.

9. Establishing Boundaries:
- Provide tools and strategies for setting healthy boundaries with emotionally immature parents.

10. Managing Anger and Resentment: - Furnish techniques for managing and processing these feelings in a healthy way.

11. Rebuilding Relationships: - Provide tips on how to rebuild or renegotiate the relationship with emotionally immature parents, if desired.

12. Therapeutic Support: - Promote the importance of therapy and how it can aid in healing.

13. Case Stories: - Share real-life examples of individuals who have faced and overcome the challenges of having emotionally immature parents.

14. Importance of Self-Care: - Offer advice on how adults can take care of themselves and their emotional needs.

15. Understanding Forgiveness: - Explore what forgiveness truly means and when it is appropriate.

16. Support Network: - Emphasize the importance of having friends, partners, or support groups that understand and provide support.

17. Impact on Personal Relationships: - Discuss how these experiences influence an adult's relationships, including partners and children.

18. Generational Awareness: - Reflect on how to break the cycle to ensure that future generations do not perpetuate the same pattern.

19. Recommended Resources and Readings: - Provide additional materials and resources for those who wish to delve deeper.

20. Exercises and Practical Techniques: - Include exercises, meditations, and techniques to help adults work on their healing.

1. Definition of Emotionally Immature Parents

Emotionally Immature Parents are individuals who, despite their chronological age, have not fully developed the capacity to adequately respond to the emotional needs of their children. This behavior does not necessarily stem from a place of malice, but often results from deficiencies in their own emotional development.

Characteristics of Emotionally Immature Parents:

1. **Self-Centeredness:** They tend to view situations based on how they personally affect them, rather than considering the needs or feelings of their children. This can lead to a lack of empathy or understanding for their children's experiences.

2. **Emotional Regulation Difficulties:** They may react excessively to minor provocations or stress, displaying anger, sadness, or other emotions inappropriately or disproportionately.

3. **Avoidance:** Some emotionally immature parents avoid conflicts or deep conversations, withdrawing or becoming defensive when pressured or feeling threatened.

4. **Need for Control:** They desire control over events and people around them, often because they internally feel powerless or insecure.

5. **Inconsistency:** They can be inconsistent in their behavior and reactions, making it difficult for children to predict or understand their responses.

6. **Denial of Reality:** They refuse to acknowledge obvious problems or accept feedback, especially if it undermines their self-image or ego.

7. **Emotional Dependence:** They rely on their children for reassurance, support, or to fulfill their own emotional needs, often reversing the parent-child role.

8. **Refusal to Admit Mistakes:** Instead of admitting an error or apologizing, they may try to blame others or justify their behavior.

However, these characteristics can vary in severity, and not all emotionally immature parents will exhibit all of these traits. It is essential to note that emotional immaturity often has roots in the parent's own childhood and life experiences. Many times, these parents did not have the opportunity or resources to address their own emotional wounds, and as a result, they cannot be emotionally present for their children in a healthy manner.

Emotionally immature parents are, in many cases, trapped in their unresolved emotional states or childhood experiences. It is a complex and multifaceted topic, and it can be helpful to further explore some of its facets.

Depth of the Issue: When we talk about emotional immaturity, we are not simply referring to a parent who occasionally shows signs of insecurity or may have an exaggerated reaction to a specific stressful event. Instead, we are describing individuals who have ingrained and consistent patterns of behavior over time, significantly influencing how they interact with their children and the world around them.

Origins of Emotional Immaturity: The roots of emotional immaturity are often deep and may extend to previous generations. Many emotionally immature parents grew up in environments where they did not learn to identify, express, or manage their emotions properly. This can be due to various reasons: a family history of trauma, emotionally distant or absent parents, or growing up in an environment where expressing emotions was seen as a sign of weakness.

Difference Between Immaturity and Disorder: It is crucial to distinguish between a parent who is simply emotionally immature and one who may have a personality disorder or another mental health issue. While there can be overlap in behaviors, the causes and potential solutions can differ significantly.

Impact on Child Development: An environment with an emotionally immature parent can lead to several challenges for the child. These children can become extremely attuned to the needs and emotions of the parent, often at the expense of their own. They may feel responsible for the well-being of the parent and may develop "parentification" behaviors, where they take on the role of a caregiver.

Implications for Identity Formation: As they grow, these children may struggle to form an autonomous identity. Because their energy has been so focused on trying to appease or take care of the parent, they may have difficulty recognizing or pursuing their own desires, needs, and aspirations.

The Cycle of Immaturity: One of the tragic ironies of the situation is that many adults who grew up with emotionally immature parents may find themselves repeating the same patterns with their own children. Without significant awareness and intervention, the cycle of immaturity can continue from generation to generation.

Navigating the Complexity of Empathy: A particular challenge in dealing with an emotionally immature parent is balancing understanding and self-preservation. On one hand, it's possible to see how a parent may have become emotionally immature due to their own challenges and traumas. This awareness can lead to a profound sense of empathy and compassion. On the other hand, it is essential to recognize and protect oneself from the harm that can result from being close to someone incapable of genuine reciprocal emotional connection. These are just some of the many dimensions surrounding the issue of emotionally immature parents. Exploring each aspect can provide a deeper understanding and help those who have been influenced by this dynamic find paths to healing and understanding.

Emotional Immaturity in Parents: It is a phenomenon that deeply affects the structure of family relationships and has complex and sometimes obscure roots. This immaturity is not simply an inability to deal with emotions; it often embodies a fusion of deficits in cognition, empathy, and self-reflection.

Interaction with the External World: Emotionally immature parents may struggle not only in their relationships with their children but also in other social contexts. This difficulty can manifest as an inability to establish deep connections with others, a sense of alienation or isolation, or a tendency to misinterpret or perceive criticism where it does not exist.

External Factors and Stress: Life's stressful events, such as job loss, financial problems, or illnesses, can exacerbate emotional immaturity. While most adults can find ways to manage stress and seek support, emotionally immature parents may become overwhelmed and may further withdraw or become more volatile.

Distorted View of Reality: A prominent trait of emotional immaturity is a distorted perception of reality. This can manifest as denial, projection, or even rewriting reality to fit an internal narrative. This distortion can confuse children, making them doubt their perception or memory of events.

Escape into Activities or Substances: It is not uncommon for emotionally immature parents to seek escape from their feelings or reality through excessive use of substances like alcohol or drugs, or through compulsive behaviors like shopping, gambling, or even excessive work.

Role of Education and Culture: Society and culture play a significant role in shaping parents' expectations and behaviors. In some cultures or contexts, showing emotions or admitting vulnerability may be seen as weak or unacceptable, further contributing to the issue of emotional immaturity.

Need for External Validation: One common trait of emotionally immature parents is their constant need for external validation. This can translate into a desire to receive praise, recognition, or any form of affirmation from others, often at the expense of their children's needs and feelings.

Impact on Child Rearing: The presence of an emotionally immature parent can profoundly influence the approach to child rearing. Children may be placed in situations where they are constantly under pressure to meet unrealistic expectations or may be neglected in terms of support and guidance.

Connection with Other Mental Issues: While emotional immaturity is a specific issue, it can coexist with a range of other mental problems, such as anxiety, depression, or even personality disorders. This comorbidity can further complicate family dynamics and the challenges that children must face.

Resilience of Children: Despite the challenges of growing up with an emotionally immature parent, many children demonstrate remarkable resilience. With the right resources and support, they can develop inner strength, deep empathy, and awareness that helps them navigate the world with grace and determination.

Emotional Immaturity, though a deep and often painful issue, also offers the opportunity for introspection, growth,

and healing for those willing to confront and work through its complex facets.
In conclusion, emotional immaturity in parents is a topic that cannot be understood or addressed superficially. This particular form of immaturity deeply impacts family dynamics and the emotional well-being of the involved children. The essence of emotional immaturity lies in deep insecurities, acquired behavior patterns, and often unresolved traumas that date back generations.

These parents, while often loving their children, struggle with a range of internal emotions that make it difficult for them to provide the stable affection, guidance, and support a child needs to develop in a healthy manner.

However, it is crucial to remember that **most emotionally immature parents do not act out of malice.** Many times, they are trapped in cycles of behavior they do not fully understand or feel they cannot escape from. Their struggle with emotional immaturity is, in most cases, a manifestation of their desire for connection, but a connection that is distorted by their own fears, insecurities, and traumas.

For the children of these parents, the road can be challenging. They may develop a series of coping strategies, some of which may serve them well, while others may become limiting in adulthood. **The key for these individuals is often awareness - by recognizing patterns, wounds, and unmet needs, they can begin the process of healing and building healthier, mutually satisfying relationships.**

In a therapeutic and supportive context, both emotionally immature parents and their children can benefit from exploring these dynamics. Therapy, education, support groups, and other resources can provide tools and insights that lead to healing and growth. Ultimately, emotional immaturity, with all its challenges, can also offer unique opportunities for deep introspection, empathy, and personal transformation.

Emotional immaturity is a concept that spans a wide range of psychological and sociocultural facets. To fully understand its origins, it is essential to examine a combination of historical, psychological, and cultural factors.

Historical Factors:

1. **Family and Generational Traumas:** In many families, unresolved past traumas can be passed down from generation to generation. These may include experiences of war, migration,

significant losses, abuse, or poverty. If these traumas are not adequately processed or understood, they can manifest as emotional immaturity in subsequent generations.

2. **Attachment History:** Attachment theory suggests that our early relationships, particularly with our primary caregivers, shape our behavior in future relationships. If an individual experienced insecure or disorganized attachment as a child, they may struggle to form healthy emotional bonds as adults.

Psychological Factors:

1. **Childhood Wounds:** Abuse, neglect, abandonment, or other forms of trauma during childhood can prevent an individual from developing full emotional maturity. These traumatic events can create an unstable foundation from which the individual operates, making it difficult to manage emotions or understand their own feelings and those of others.

2. **Personality Disorders:** Certain disorders, such as borderline personality disorder or narcissistic personality disorder, can manifest with traits of emotional immaturity. While not all

individuals with emotional immaturity have a personality disorder, there is overlap in behaviors and dynamics.

3. **Fear of Intimacy:** Some individuals may have a fear of intimacy due to past experiences. This fear can manifest as a reluctance to share deep emotions, creating a barrier between them and their loved ones.

Cultural Factors:

1. **Sociocultural Norms:** In some cultures, openly expressing emotions may be viewed as a sign of weakness. People are often encouraged to suppress their emotions or mask them, leading to an inability to manage them adequately or emotionally relate to others.

2. **Gender Roles:** In many societies, there are rigid expectations regarding how each gender should behave emotionally. For example, men may be discouraged from showing vulnerability, while women may be seen as "emotionally unstable" if they express anger. These stereotypes can hinder healthy emotional development.

3. **Pressure of Modern Society:** We live in an era of constant connectivity, stress, and rapid changes. The pressure to conform, succeed, and "have it all" can lead people to ignore or deny

their own emotions to maintain an appearance of control or competence.

Understanding the origins of emotional immaturity requires a holistic view that takes into account the multiple factors influencing an individual's emotional development. Only through this multidimensional lens can we hope to address, heal, and prevent emotional immaturity in future generations.

Emotional immaturity, when examined through a multidisciplinary lens, reveals profound and layered complexity, enriched by a series of influences. While the listed factors are central, there are other nuances that contribute to the formation of this trait.

Firstly, biology plays a role. Neurochemistry and brain structure can influence how a person perceives, processes, and responds to emotions. For instance, if the brain areas responsible for emotional regulation are not fully developed or are affected by chemical imbalances, emotionally immature behaviors may emerge. Additionally, some studies have suggested that genetic predisposition may make certain individuals more susceptible to emotional immaturity, especially when exposed to certain environments or stressors.

Another significant aspect is observational learning. Humans are naturally inclined to imitate and model the behavior of those around them, especially during their childhood and adolescence. If a child grows up observing adults (not necessarily their parents) handling their emotions in an unhealthy or immature manner, they are likely to adopt similar behaviors, believing them to be normative or acceptable.

Social dynamics and friendships can also contribute to emotional immaturity. Individuals who find themselves in groups where emotional immaturity is valued or normalized—such as environments where shallowness, manipulation, or instability are common—may adapt to conform, developing habits and behaviors that reflect these norms.

Life experiences, especially those interpreted as failures or rejections, can reinforce emotional immaturity in some individuals. If a person has experienced repeated setbacks or rejections and has not learned to cope with or glean lessons from them, they may become emotionally stunted, avoiding future emotional risks or reacting disproportionately to minor challenges or setbacks.

Literature, media, and modern technologies can have both positive and negative roles. On one hand, access to information and resources on mental and emotional health can provide tools for developing greater emotional maturity. On the other hand, excessive use of social media, information overload, and the constant need to compare oneself with others can fuel insecurities, anxieties, and reduced capacity for introspection and deep reflection—factors that can contribute to emotional immaturity.

In conclusion, the roots of emotional immaturity are deeply intertwined in a web of individual experiences, environmental influences, and innate predispositions.

The environment in which an individual grows up significantly impacts their emotional maturity development. Take, for example, educational contexts. If school environments do not promote emotional competence, children may not learn to recognize, express, or manage their emotions appropriately. Interactions with peers, teachers, and the curriculum itself can shape how a young person will perceive and respond to emotional challenges throughout life.

Similarly, exposure to conflict situations, such as neighborhoods or families with high levels of violence, can influence emotional immaturity. In environments where survival and safety are at stake, emotions may be quickly suppressed or distorted for self-preservation. This could be a completely logical reaction to the environment, but in less severe situations or in adulthood, these patterns may appear as emotional immaturity.

Another aspect to consider is the cultural approach to mental health in general. In many cultures, mental health remains a taboo, and people may lack the resources or knowledge to address their own emotional challenges. Without adequate language or understanding to express and manage emotions, these individuals may appear emotionally immature when, in reality, they may simply lack the tools or education to deal with their emotions.

Modern technology and the fast-paced nature of contemporary life also impact emotional immaturity. Instant gratification provided by technology can hinder an individual's ability to develop patience, tolerance, and resilience. When people are accustomed to getting immediate answers and results, they may not know how to cope with waiting, disappointment, or frustration, all of which require a certain level of maturity to handle properly.

Furthermore, the lack of authenticity in online interactions can lead to a lack of empathy and understanding. If an individual spends most of their time in virtual environments, they may not fully develop the ability to read others' emotions, express themselves authentically, or create deep and meaningful connections.

Finally, the ongoing pressure to present a "perfect version" of oneself, often amplified by social media, can lead to a lack of authenticity and an inability to confront imperfections and vulnerabilities, both in oneself and others. This pressure to conform to an often unattainable ideal can further contribute to emotional immaturity.

In conclusion, the origin of emotional immaturity is a complex and intrinsic combination of biological, environmental, psychological, and sociocultural influences. An individual's emotional development trajectory is like a mosaic, composed of a multitude of pieces coming together to form a larger picture.

On one hand, we have biological factors such as neurochemistry, brain structure, and genetic predispositions, which can provide a foundation for how emotions are perceived and managed. These elements, if not balanced or negatively influenced by external factors, can predispose an individual to emotional immaturity.
On the other hand, environmental influences, such as education, life experiences, and social interactions, continuously shape and mold this biological foundation. Growing up in an unstable or traumatic environment, or simply one that

does not value or teach healthy emotional management, can divert healthy emotional development. The pressures of modern society, amplified by technology and media, can further complicate this journey, pushing individuals toward emotional immaturity as a defense mechanism or as a result of instant gratification and unrealistic expectations.

Cultural and societal influences, with their norms, values, and taboos, serve as the backdrop to all of this, directly or indirectly influencing how emotions are perceived, expressed, and valued. Cultural norms can both suppress emotional maturity through rigid expectations and gender stereotypes and promote it through the celebration of emotional diversity and encouragement of authenticity.

Recognizing emotional immaturity and its multifactorial origins is the crucial first step in addressing it. Only with a deep and comprehensive understanding of the roots of this phenomenon can we hope to provide appropriate solutions, interventions, and support to those affected, allowing them to embark on a path toward greater emotional maturity and mental health.

3. **The Impact of Emotional Immaturity on Childhood**: Analyzing how children grow up in an environment with emotionally immature parents.

The emotional immaturity of parents has profound repercussions on the psychological, emotional, and relational development of children. When a parent is unable to adequately respond to a child's emotional needs, complex dynamics can be triggered that influence the child's self-perception, trust in relationships, and ability to manage their own emotions.

1. Insecure Attachment: One fundamental aspect of childhood is the development of a secure attachment to primary caregivers. Children develop a basic sense of security when they know they can rely on their parents for comfort and protection. Emotionally immature parents may be inconsistent in their responses, leading children to develop either anxious or avoidant attachments. These children may become overly concerned about the security of their relationships or may avoid intimacy to protect themselves from potential rejection.

2. Low Self-Esteem: Lack of emotional responsiveness or inconsistency from parents can make children feel unloved or unwanted. This perception can evolve into low self-esteem and feelings of inadequacy. The child may begin to believe that there is something fundamentally wrong with them because their emotional needs are not met.

3. Difficulty in Emotion Regulation: Children learn to manage their emotions through modeling and interaction with parents. If a parent is emotionally immature, they may not provide the child with the necessary tools to understand, express, and regulate their own emotions. This can lead to episodes of anger, anxiety, sadness, or withdrawal.

4. Lack of Social Skills: Interaction with an emotionally available parent helps children develop social skills such as empathy, sharing, and listening. An environment devoid of such interactions can make it difficult for the child to learn and practice these skills in other contexts, such as school or with peers.

5. External Validation Seeking: In the absence of validation and recognition from parents, a child may constantly seek approval and validation from external sources, becoming overly preoccupied with pleasing others or conforming to external expectations at the expense of their own needs and desires.

6. Dysfunctional Relational Patterns: Growing up in an environment with emotionally immature parents, children may develop relational patterns that reflect these initial dynamics. This may manifest as a tendency to form relationships with partners who replicate the same patterns of distance, rejection, or inconsistency.

7. Mental Health Risks: Prolonged exposure to an emotionally unresponsive environment can increase the risk of developing mental health problems such as depression, anxiety, eating disorders, or addiction.

In summary, while children are incredibly resilient, growing up in an environment with emotionally immature parents can pose significant challenges. Understanding these dynamics and implementing appropriate interventions and support can help children navigate these difficult environments and develop greater emotional maturity and long-term well-being.

The family environment serves as the first laboratory for social and emotional learning. Daily interactions with parents, or those in their role, offer children their first lessons on how to perceive themselves, others, and the world around them. When these parents are emotionally immature, the teachings conveyed can often be distorted or inconsistent.

For example, in families where parents do not acknowledge or minimize their children's emotions, the children may grow up without the ability to recognize or label their own emotions. In such circumstances, children may develop a form of "emotional illiteracy," finding it difficult to identify and differentiate between various emotions. This deficiency can lead to difficulties in recognizing and appropriately responding to the emotions of others, a key skill in building healthy interpersonal relationships.

In addition to the lack of emotional recognition, exposure to unpredictable or volatile behaviors from parents can lead children to develop a constant state of alertness. In these families, the environment may be perceived as unstable or unpredictable, causing children to live in a state of constant vigilance or anxiety. This state of hypervigilance can affect their academic performance, their ability to build friendships, and their overall well-being.

Another consequence of growing up with emotionally immature parents is the tendency to reverse roles. In some circumstances, the child may feel obligated to take care of the parent, assuming responsibilities that go beyond their age or capabilities. This can occur when the parent overly relies on the child for emotional support or when the child feels they must "protect" the parent from negative emotions. This dynamic can deprive the child of a true childhood, forcing them to mature too quickly and take on responsibilities that should not be theirs.

Furthermore, children raised in these environments may develop a distorted view of love and acceptance. They may believe that love is conditional, based on performance or conforming to others' expectations. This perception can lead to seeking relationships in which they constantly feel undervalued or in which they believe they must constantly "earn" love and approval from others.

Lastly, exposure to rejection or emotional withdrawal behaviors from parents can instill in children a profound fear of abandonment. This fear can manifest in various ways, such as insecurity in relationships, jealousy, or difficulty trusting others. The fear of abandonment can lead to either overly clingy behavior or, conversely, to detachment, depending on how the child chooses to cope with this anxiety.

The dynamics between emotionally immature parents and their children can influence the development of fundamental skills for the child. For example, problem-solving and conflict resolution skills are often influenced by how parents handle stressful situations. If a parent responds to challenges with emotional withdrawal, denial, or irrational outbursts, a child may not develop effective and mature methods for dealing with difficulties.

Resilience, the ability to bounce back quickly from adversity, can also be influenced. Children need role models who demonstrate how to face challenges with strength and determination. In the absence of these models, children may grow up feeling powerless in the face of adversity or may not learn to see challenges as opportunities for growth.

The concept of boundaries is another fundamental element that may not be well-developed in children with emotionally immature parents. Children learn the notion of personal boundaries through interactions with parents and other family members. When a parent does not respect a child's emotional or physical boundaries, this can lead to difficulties in establishing and maintaining healthy boundaries in future relationships. The child may grow up believing that it is normal for their needs to be constantly set aside or that it is acceptable to invade others' personal space.

The sense of reality and perception of the world can also be distorted in the presence of emotionally immature parents. For example, if a parent constantly denies responsibility or reframes reality to suit their own needs or perceptions, a child may struggle to distinguish between what is real and what is distorted. This can lead to confusion, anxiety, and a lack of confidence in their own perceptions.

The formation of identity is another crucial process during childhood and adolescence. Children seek to understand who they are, what their place in the world is, and what makes them unique. This quest for identity can be hindered if parents do not provide positive feedback or if they manipulate or belittle the child's achievements and feelings. In such circumstances, a child may develop an identity based on seeking to please others or avoiding conflict, rather than on a true understanding of themselves.

Lastly, the ability to experience joy and appreciate the small things in life can be compromised. Children have an innate sense of wonder and curiosity. However, in an environment where positive feelings are often suppressed or ridiculed, or where there is a lack of enthusiasm or appreciation for daily joys, this capacity for wonderment can diminish or, in the worst cases, disappear altogether.

The essence of childhood is intertwined with self-discovery, learning about relationships with others, and understanding one's place in the world. These developmental processes are profoundly influenced by the environment in which a child grows up, and parents, as the most influential figures in this phase, play a crucial role.

In the presence of emotionally immature parents, many of these developmental milestones can be deviated or disrupted. The damage is not always immediately visible; often, the repercussions of a childhood spent with emotionally immature parents only emerge in adulthood when the individual encounters difficulties in relationships, emotional management, or defining their own identity.

One of the most painful aspects of having emotionally immature parents is the potential loss of what could have been. Every child deserves a childhood in which they feel seen, heard, and understood. While many children find ways to adapt and develop coping mechanisms, the shadow of what was missing can persist. This sense of "lack" may manifest as a constant search for approval, a struggle to establish deep and meaningful relationships, or a feeling of disconnection from one's true identity. Furthermore, an individual's ability to form secure and affectionate bonds can be compromised. Secure attachment, formed through consistent and loving interactions with caregivers during childhood, lays the foundation for future relationships. In the absence of this attachment, a person may develop insecure attachment patterns that can lead to problematic relational dynamics in adulthood.

However, it is essential to note that not all children who grow up with emotionally immature parents are destined for problematic or unsatisfying lives. Many find the strength and resources, both internal and external, to overcome these initial challenges. Some seek therapeutic support or find support in other positive adult figures in their lives, such as teachers, relatives, or mentors.

In conclusion, while childhood is a formative and vulnerable period, it is also a time of great resilience. The impact of having emotionally immature parents can be profound and lasting, but with the right guidance, support, and understanding, it is possible to rewrite one's story, find healing, and build a bright and meaningful future.

4. Signs and Symptoms in Children: Identify typical behaviors and signs of children living in these conditions.

The presence of emotionally immature parents can influence the behavior and emotional well-being of children in various ways. While each child is an individual and may react differently to circumstances, there are some common signs and symptoms that may emerge in children living with parents incapable of providing adequate emotional support. Here is a detailed overview of such behaviors and signs:

1. **Regression Behavior:** A child may revert to bchaviors associated with an earlier developmental stage, such as thumb-sucking, tantrums, or issues with bladder control.
2. **Social Withdrawal:** The child may isolate themselves, showing little interest in interacting with peers or adults outside the family.
3. **Anxiety and Excessive Worry:** Evident through nervous behaviors, constant worries, or anxious questions about the future.
4. **Sleep and Eating:** Sleep disturbances like nightmares, night terrors, or insomnia may manifest. Appetite could also be affected, leading to overeating or undereating.
5. **Low Self-Esteem:** The child may speak negatively about themselves, show reluctance to

try new things, or express beliefs like "I'm not good enough."

6. **School Problems:** Concentration difficulties, declining academic performance, or problematic behaviors at school may become evident.
7. **Excessive Attachment or Dependence:** The child might become overly clingy, struggling to separate from parents or other significant figures.
8. **Self-Destructive Behaviors:** In severe cases, some children may start displaying self-destructive behaviors like self-harm or discussing suicidal thoughts.
9. **Feelings of Anger or Frustration:** These can manifest through anger outbursts, violent behaviors, or oppositional behavior.
10. **Trust Issues:** Difficulty in forming bonds with others, distrust, or fear of adults.
11. **Feelings of Loneliness:** Even when surrounded by others, these children may express feelings of isolation or being misunderstood.
12. **Mimicry or Overadaptation:** In an attempt to avoid conflict or gain attention, the child may try to "disappear" by blending into the environment or over-adapting to others' needs, often at the expense of their own.
13. **Escape into Fantasy:** To compensate for the emotionally deficient environment, the child

might develop imaginary worlds or become excessively immersed in books, movies, or video games as a means of escape.

14. **Excessive Responsibility:** Some children may attempt to "fix" the situation by taking on responsibilities beyond their age, such as caring for younger siblings or trying to mediate between parents.

In summary, children living with emotionally immature parents can display a wide range of signs and symptoms due to the emotionally deficient environment. However, it is crucial to remember that these signs are not a life sentence; with adequate support and timely intervention, children can overcome these challenges and thrive.

Continuing the analysis of signs and symptoms in children raised by emotionally immature parents, it is important to emphasize that the context and individuality of the children can influence how these signs manifest.

Some of the signs may be subtle and less obvious, while others could be extremely evident. Here are further details and facets of this issue:

1. **Somatization**: Children may develop physical symptoms in response to emotional stress. This can include headaches, stomachaches, or other

pains and disorders without an apparent medical cause.

2. **Avoidance of Responsibility**: In contrast to those who take excessive responsibility, some children may completely avoid responsibilities, refusing to tackle any task or challenge.

3. **Excessive Dependence on Electronic Devices**: In an attempt to distract or escape from reality, some children may become overly attached to their electronic devices, such as smartphones or computers, spending hours on activities like online gaming.

4. **Fear of Criticism**: They might avoid situations where they fear being judged or criticized, as every little critique could be experienced as confirmation of their inner fears of inadequacy.

5. **Difficulty Expressing Emotions**: They may struggle to identify or talk about their own feelings, often keeping everything inside until they can no longer contain it.

6. **Approval Seeking**: Some children may constantly seek approval and reassurance from adults and peers, often altering their behavior to please others at the expense of their authenticity.

7. **Jealousy of Peers**: Since these children may notice the difference between their families and those of their friends, they may feel envy or jealousy toward peers they perceive as having a "normal" or "better" family life.

8. **Avoidance of Intimacy**: Growing up in an environment where emotional intimacy is not modeled or valued can lead the child to avoid or fear intimacy in future relationships.

9. **Perfectionism**: In an effort to avoid criticism or rejection, the child may develop perfectionistic traits, putting pressure on themselves to be the best at everything they do.

10. **Feelings of Helplessness**: They may feel as if they have no control over their life or destiny, leading to feelings of despair and apathy. It is essential to remember that while these signs may indicate the presence of emotionally immature parents, they can also be influenced by a myriad of other factors. Every child is an individual, and their reactions and behaviors will be a unique mix of temperament, experiences, and environmental context. Additionally, a child may only exhibit some of these signs or manifest them differently from described. The key is careful observation and listening, providing the child with a safe environment in which they can express and process their emotions and concerns. The environment in which a child grows up plays a fundamental role in shaping their behavior, self-perception, and ability to relate to others. The presence of emotionally immature parents can have profound and lasting impacts that go beyond immediately visible signs.

Let's explore additional aspects that may surface in children exposed to these dynamics:

1. **Emotional Ambivalence**: Children may develop ambivalent feelings towards their parents, swinging between a desire for closeness and feelings of anger or resentment. They may also struggle to reconcile these conflicting emotions.

2. **Dependency on Rigid Family Roles**: To seek predictability and structure in an unstable environment, the child may rigidly adhere to a specific role within the family, such as peacemaker, rebel, or caretaker.

3. **Hypervigilance**: Growing up in an unpredictable environment, the child can develop a constant sense of alertness, always ready to react to potential threats or changes.

4. **Difficulty Establishing Boundaries**: They might struggle to differentiate themselves from others, finding it hard to assert their needs or say "no" to others' requests.

5. **Compulsive Behaviors**: As a coping mechanism, compulsive behaviors may develop, such as repeatedly washing hands, obsessively checking things, or hoarding objects.

6. **Pervasive Sense of Shame**: Even in the absence of apparent reasons, the child may feel

deeply inadequate or ashamed of themselves, believing they are fundamentally flawed.

7. **Tendency to Ruminate**: They may spend a lot of time reflecting on past events, trying to make sense of their experiences or worrying about the future.

8. **Desire for Normalcy**: A profound desire for "normalcy" may emerge, with the child attempting to blend in or conform to social expectations while never truly feeling "normal."

9. **Inhibited Creativity**: The fear of expressing themselves freely and the dread of judgment may inhibit them from showcasing their creativity or pursuing artistic passions.

10. **Relationship with the Body**: Issues like eating disorders, body dissatisfaction, or disconnection from their own bodies can develop as a result of emotional tension and lack of acceptance.

11. **Tendency to Form Toxic Relationships**: Growing up without proper models of healthy interaction, the child may repeat toxic family patterns in their future relationships.

The list of potential signs and behaviors in children with emotionally immature parents may seem daunting, but it is essential to understand the breadth and depth of the impact such parents can have. However, it's also important to note that not all of these signs will appear in every child, and there are effective therapeutic resources and interventions that can help both children and adults heal and build healthier relationships.

The complexity of the signs and symptoms that emerge in children raised by emotionally immature parents underscores the interplay between the family context and the child's development. Growing up in an environment characterized by emotional instability, lack of empathy, and a failure to understand the child's needs can, in many cases, lead to a range of behavioral and psychological responses in children. These signs are not merely symptomatic of a single issue; instead, they are manifestations of a series of interconnected problems stemming from a deficient growth environment.

Each symptom or sign that emerges in a child should not be viewed in isolation but rather as part of a complex network of responses and coping strategies the child has developed to navigate their environment. For example, the tendency to ruminate may be linked to a pervasive sense of shame or hypervigilance, while rigid adherence to family roles might result from the child's attempts to bring order and predictability to a chaotic environment.

The depth and breadth of these signs and symptoms highlight the importance of early intervention and adequate support. While it is true that many children can demonstrate resilience and adaptability, this does not mean they do not need help or that their experiences have not left scars. On the contrary, resilience and adaptability can sometimes mask the true need for support, understanding, and therapy. In conclusion, it is essential to recognize that the emotional immaturity of parents not only impacts daily family dynamics but also has long-term repercussions on the psycho-emotional development of children. Recognizing these signs is the crucial first step in providing the necessary support and embarking on a healing journey. Therapy, school support, positive interactions with trusted adults, and a deep understanding of their experiences can help these children navigate life's challenges and build a healthy and fulfilling future. The key is empathy, understanding, and informed action to help these children recognize their worth and rebuild confidence in themselves and the world around them.

5. Long-Term Repercussions: Explore how these childhood issues influence adulthood in terms of relationships, career, and overall well-being.

Childhood experiences, especially those related to the nature of parent-child relationships, leave an indelible imprint that can profoundly influence an individual's adult life. Dynamics established during childhood can manifest in various ways, impacting relationships, careers, and overall well-being. Let's explore some of the most significant long-term repercussions that growing up with emotionally immature parents can have on the adult individual:

1. **Interpersonal Relationships:** Adults who had emotionally immature parents may struggle to establish and maintain intimate relationships. They may fear rejection, have difficulty trusting others, or avoid closeness for fear of being hurt. At the same time, they may also find themselves in toxic relationships, replicating family dynamics they experienced as children.
2. **Self-Esteem:** These adults may have low self-esteem, often rooted in childhood experiences where they felt misunderstood, neglected, or rejected. The persistent feeling of not being

"good enough" can influence life decisions and personal aspirations.

3. **Career and Professional Achievements:** Fear of judgment, performance anxiety, and a tendency toward self-sabotage can hinder professional progress. Simultaneously, some may become overly ambitious or perfectionistic, seeking to compensate for perceived shortcomings or seeking approval and validation through external successes.

4. **Mental Health:** Exposure to emotionally immature parents can increase the risk of developing mental health issues such as depression, anxiety, eating disorders, or addictions. These problems can be attempts to manage or mask the pain and confusion stemming from childhood trauma.

5. **Emotional Regulation:** Adults may struggle to identify, express, and manage their own emotions. This may manifest as excessive reactivity, emotional withdrawal, or the use of unhealthy defense mechanisms to avoid emotional pain.

6. **Life Choices and Coping:** To compensate for a childhood lacking support, some may seek comfort in destructive behaviors such as substance abuse, fleeting relationships, or gambling.

7. **Self-Perception and Worldview:** Self-image can be distorted, with adults seeing themselves through a negative lens. Their view of the world can become defensive or cynical, influencing their ability to build positive relationships and hope for a better future.
8. **Body and Physical Well-Being:** The accumulation of emotional stress and trauma can also manifest physically, leading to issues like insomnia, eating disorders, chronic muscle tension, or stress-related illnesses.
9. **Fear of Change and Growth:** The familiarity of childhood dynamics, even if negative, can make some adults reluctant to change, fearing the unknown or the possibility of failure.
10. **Need for Control:** Having experienced a chaotic environment during childhood, adults may seek excessive control over their surroundings, leading to dysfunctional relational dynamics or obsessive-compulsive behaviors.

In conclusion, the long-term repercussions of a childhood spent with emotionally immature parents are profound and multifaceted. However, it is crucial to emphasize that, despite these challenges, many adults find paths to healing and growth. Therapy, self-reflection, supportive relationships, and the acquisition of new coping skills can help individuals overcome these obstacles and build a fulfilling life.

The implications of being raised by emotionally immature parents can radiate into nearly every aspect of an individual's life. While the primary consequences have already been explored, there are many layers and facets of this impact that warrant further reflection:

Attitude and Communication Styles: Adults raised in families with emotionally immature parents may have developed specific ways of communicating and relating to others. They might exhibit passive-aggressive behaviors, as they may never have learned how to openly express frustration or discomfort. Alternatively, they might completely avoid conflicts, withdrawing or acquiescing in the face of any form of tension. This can lead to relationships where their own needs and desires are consistently sidelined.

View of Intimacy: Intimacy, both emotional and physical, may be seen as something dangerous or threatening. This is because past openness and vulnerability with parents may have led to rejection or ridicule. As a result, the idea of becoming intimate with someone, even in a romantic relationship, can evoke anxiety or fear.

Dependency and Independence: The swinging dynamic between desiring independence and fearing isolation can become a central struggle. Some may become excessively independent, refusing help even when they need it, while others may become overly dependent, continually seeking reassurance and approval from others.

Seeking Alternative Parental Roles: A common tendency among those who had emotionally immature parents is to seek substitute parental figures in adulthood. This can manifest by seeking mentors, older friends, or even therapists who can provide the guidance and support that was lacking during childhood.

Self-Perception of Worth: Many adults may base their sense of worth on what they do rather than who they are. This can lead to an excessive emphasis on achievements and external success as a measure of self-esteem.

Stress Management and Resilience: The ability to manage stress and recover from adverse events may be compromised. Situations that might seem trivial or manageable to others can feel overwhelming for those who grew up in an unstable environment.

Learning and Growth Modes: The approach to learning and personal growth might be influenced by a fear of making mistakes or exposing one's "inadequacy." This can lead to avoiding new experiences or challenges, limiting one's capacity for growth and development.

Sensitivity to Others' Needs: Paradoxically, while their own emotional growth may have been hindered, many adults with emotionally immature parents develop deep sensitivity to the needs and feelings of others. They may become extremely empathetic, often at the expense of their own needs and boundaries.

Perception of Family and Parenthood: When becoming parents themselves, adults with a history of emotionally immature parents may be highly determined to "break the cycle" and provide their children with what they lacked. However, without adequate reflection and therapy, they may unconsciously repeat some learned behaviors.

These are just some of the many ways growing up in an environment with emotionally immature parents can influence an individual's life. While the challenges are significant, with the right introspection, support, and resources, it is possible to find healing and build a rich and fulfilling life.

Insecure Attachment Style: One of the most profound implications of being raised by emotionally immature parents is the development of insecure attachment styles. Attachment styles form in response to how a child's emotional needs are met by their caregivers. When caregivers are unpredictable, distant, or overly invasive, children may develop anxious, avoidant, or disorganized attachment styles. These attachment patterns can deeply influence how an individual approaches relationships in adulthood, often leading to unhealthy dynamics.

Tendency Toward Toxic Relationships: Given their past experience, adults who grew up with emotionally immature parents may find it challenging to recognize and establish healthy relationships. They might be drawn to partners who replicate family behaviors, even if they are harmful, or they may struggle to establish healthy boundaries.

Dissociation and Escapism: To cope with the emotional instability of childhood, some may have developed defense mechanisms like dissociation. This involves detaching from the surrounding reality, often as a reaction to stressful or traumatic situations. In adulthood, this dissociation can manifest in various ways, such as the inability to stay present in emotionally charged situations or a tendency to mentally "escape."

Self-Sabotage: Low self-esteem and self-confidence can lead to self-sabotaging behaviors. This may include avoiding opportunities that would lead to success, withdrawing from promising relationships, or creating problems in otherwise stable situations. Self-sabotage can stem from the unconscious belief that one is unworthy of happiness or success.

Hypersensitivity to Criticism: Growing up in an environment where self-esteem was constantly compromised can make individuals extremely sensitive to criticism. This hypersensitivity can manifest by avoiding situations where they might be judged or by reacting excessively to even constructive feedback.

Compulsions and Addictions: To cope with unresolved pain, some may turn to compulsive behaviors or addictions. This could involve substance use, binge-eating, compulsive shopping, or any behavior that provides temporary relief from inner turmoil.

Identity Issues: Without a solid model of self-reference and emotional understanding during childhood, many people struggle to develop a clear sense of self. This lack of a clear identity can lead to a continual search for belonging and external approval.

Parenting Challenges: When individuals become parents, the wounds and deficiencies from their childhood can resurface. This might manifest through uncertainty about their ability to be good parents or through the unconscious repetition of behaviors learned from their own parents.

The depth and breadth of long-term implications are vast, and each individual will have their unique combination of challenges and reactions based on their personal experiences. However, recognizing these patterns and understanding their origins is the crucial first step toward healing and creating a healthier and more satisfying life.

Understanding the long-term repercussions of growing up with emotionally immature parents is essential not only for those who have directly experienced these situations but also for mental health professionals, educators, and society as a whole. The weaving of the multiple challenges described offers a detailed look at how a childhood devoid of emotional stability can influence identity formation, how people perceive themselves and others, and how they navigate challenges in adulthood.

Being raised by emotionally immature parents can trigger a series of self-protective behaviors and distorted thought patterns. While these behaviors and patterns may have made sense during childhood as adaptation mechanisms in an unpredictable environment, they often do not serve the individual well in their adult life and can become obstacles to well-being and happiness.

Relationships can become particularly problematic, as individuals may unconsciously seek familiar family dynamics in adults or struggle with vulnerability and intimacy due to past wounds. Career, education, and other aspects of life can be influenced by deep-seated insecurities, self-sabotage, and hypersensitivity to criticism.

However, with a profound awareness of the origins of these challenges and a commitment to healing, there is hope. Many individuals overcome their initial difficulties and build lives full of meaning, connection, and fulfillment. The importance of therapeutic support, support communities, and educational resources cannot be stressed enough—they are essential in helping people dismantle old patterns and build new strategies for a satisfying life.

Human resilience is extraordinary, and while childhood wounds can leave deep scars, the capacity for healing, growth, and transformation is equally profound. The key lies in recognition, acceptance, and active pursuit of change and support.

The Role of Money and Power: In many families, money and power are closely intertwined and can be used as means to exert control, influence family dynamics, and manifest insecurities or emotional immaturity. When it comes to emotionally immature parents, this connection can become particularly evident and problematic.

1. **Control through Economic Resources:** Emotionally immature parents may use money as a tool of manipulation. This can include threats to withdraw financial support, giving money or goods as a form of manipulation, or excessively controlling their children's expenses, even when they are adults.

2. **Money as a Substitute for Affection:** In some families, gifts, money, or other forms of material support can substitute genuine affection and emotional attention. Instead of providing empathy, understanding, and emotional support, an emotionally immature parent may resort to purchasing goods as a clumsy attempt to "fix" emotional problems or as a means to show love.

3. **Insecurity and Display:** Emotional insecurity can lead to a need for ostentation or excessive spending as an attempt to gain social approval or bolster one's self-esteem. A parent may try to impress others through material possessions, trying to compensate for their emotional deficiencies.

4. **Impulsive Financial Decisions:** Emotional immaturity can manifest through impulsive or irresponsible financial decisions. Instead of considering long-term implications or the family's overall needs, an emotionally immature parent might make purchases based on immediate emotional needs or fleeting desires.

5. **Power as a Means of Control:** In addition to money, power in the form of authority or control can be wielded in unhealthy ways. This might manifest as a need to dominate or control family decisions, restrict the autonomy of other family members, or use guilt and manipulation to maintain a dominant position.

6. **Avoidance of Responsibility:** Paradoxically, while some emotionally immature parents may seek to excessively control finances and power decisions, others may avoid financial responsibilities, neglecting the family's needs or entrusting money management to others without adequate reflection or understanding.

7. **Conflicts and Rivalry:** Emotional immaturity can lead to conflicts related to money and power within the family, with individual members competing for resources or feeling threatened when others gain financial autonomy or power. In conclusion, money and power, in the hands of emotionally immature individuals, can become tools of manipulation, control, and conflict within the family. The ability to recognize and address these unhealthy dynamics is essential to break cycles of dependency, manipulation, and abuse. Awareness of the emotional motivations behind financial and power decisions can help individuals navigate and build healthier and more balanced family relationships. Understanding how money and power are used within a family dominated by emotionally immature parents provides a deep insight into the patterns of behavior that can emerge.

   The Scarcity Dynamics: In certain contexts, emotionally immature parents can create an environment of scarcity, where there's a constant perception that there's never enough money, regardless of the family's actual financial situation. This can instill a scarcity mindset in children, leading them to constantly fear not having enough, both in terms of material resources and emotional resources.

Personal Worth Tied to Material Possessions: When emotional capabilities are lacking, an individual's worth may be perceived as tightly linked to their material possessions. This can result in self-imposed pressure on oneself and other family members to achieve material success as a means to earn love and approval.

Money as an Emotion Substitute: In moments of tension or conflict, an emotionally immature parent might offer money or gifts as a way to "fix" the situation, rather than addressing the true emotional issue. This can lead children to develop an unhealthy relationship with money, viewing it as a substitute for affection or as a means to gain parental approval.

Financial Dependency and Autonomy: In some families, an emotionally immature parent may deliberately keep their children in a state of financial dependency, preventing them from acquiring the skills and confidence needed to become independent. This financial control can become a tool to keep children "close," both emotionally and physically, well into adulthood.

Avoidance and Denial: Conversely, some emotionally immature parents may completely avoid money issues, living in a state of denial regarding their financial responsibilities. This can lead to problems such as unpaid debts, irrational spending, or avoidance of significant financial decisions that impact the entire family.

Resonance in Future Relationships: Children raised in these dynamics may carry unhealthy patterns into their adult lives. For example, they might seek partners who exert financial control over them, or conversely, they might completely avoid money and financial responsibilities in their relationships.

Indeed, when parents use money as an extension of their insecurities or as a means to exert control, this can have profound repercussions on the emotional and financial development of their children. These patterns can run deep, influencing not only how an individual views money but also how they perceive themselves and their value within relationships.

Financial Abuse and Relationships: An extreme manifestation of money and power manipulation is financial abuse, where a parent or partner uses money as a tool to control and dominate the other. They may restrict access to funds, control all financial decisions, or use money as a means to punish or reward.

The Inheritance Question: In families with emotionally immature parents, the issue of inheritance can become a minefield. Promises, threats of disinheritance, and manipulations may surround the concept of who will receive what, making money and assets a central point of tension and conflict.

Distorted Values: Due to an excessive focus on money and power, children can grow up believing that material success is the only measure of success in life. This may lead them to pursue material goals at the expense of relationships, happiness, and personal fulfillment.

Undervaluing Money: Some emotionally immature parents, in an attempt to appear non-materialistic, may downplay the value and importance of money, causing children to lack a healthy understanding of personal finance and self-sufficiency.

Status Importance: In some families, money is seen as a means to gain social status. This can lead to an excessive concern for appearances, branding, and ostentation, imparting upon children the idea that their worth depends on what they possess or how they are perceived by others.

Fear of Rejection: If parents use money as a means of approval, children can develop a deep fear of rejection tied to financial stability. They may feel loved only when financially prosperous or as if they must "buy" love and approval through gifts and spending.

Relationship between Self-esteem and Finances: Growing up in an environment where money is closely tied to self-esteem, children can develop a distorted sense of their own worth. They may feel inadequate if they fail to achieve certain financial goals or if they cannot maintain a particular lifestyle.

Financial Risk-Taking Behavior: Due to emotional instability and a lack of healthy financial education, some children raised in these contexts may become adults who engage in risky financial behaviors, such as impulsive spending, accumulating debt, or investing in high-risk schemes.

The complexities of money and power dynamics in families with emotionally immature parents are profound and far-reaching. While each family is unique, there are common patterns that can emerge when emotional immaturity intersects with financial and power-related decisions.

Money, at its core, is a tool, a medium of exchange that facilitates transactions and represents value in a society. However, in the dynamics of a family where emotionally immature parents prevail, money goes far beyond its basic function, transforming into a tool of control, power, manipulation, and, in some cases, abuse.

In families with emotionally immature parents, money can become the epicenter of many tensions. It can be used as a mechanism to exert control, where access to funds is limited or used as a means to manipulate emotions and behaviors. In this dynamic, children can grow up seeing money not only as a resource but as a symbol of love, approval, or even as a barometer of their intrinsic worth.

The distorted use of money can have profound repercussions. For instance, a child raised in an environment where love is "purchased" through gifts or approval is earned through material success can develop a skewed view of their self-esteem. These individuals might begin to tie their sense of identity and worth to material possessions or financial success rather than to intrinsic qualities such as kindness, compassion, or intelligence.

Furthermore, when an emotionally immature parent uses money as the primary means of interaction with their children, it can deprive them of the opportunity to develop healthy emotional skills. Instead of learning to communicate, understand, and confront their own emotions and those of others, these children learn that money is the only language that matters—a language that can easily silence conflicts but rarely resolves the underlying issues.

In conclusion, money and power, when used in a distorted manner within the family, can create a toxic and warped environment. It is crucial to recognize these patterns and work to break them, ensuring that future generations can have a healthy view of money, power, and interpersonal relationships. The key lies in education, awareness, and support—providing individuals with the resources and tools necessary to decipher, understand, and ultimately resolve these intricate entanglements of emotions and finances.

7. Coping Strategies: Explore the tactics children adopt to cope, such as denial, isolation, or conformity.

When children grow up in an environment with emotionally immature parents, they often develop a series of coping strategies to navigate this complicated and sometimes harmful context. These strategies can vary based on the child's personality, specific circumstances, and the extent of the parents' emotional immaturity. Let's examine some of these strategies:

1. **Denial:** This is one of the first defenses a child may develop. By refusing to acknowledge or accept that there is a problem, the child may temporarily feel safe. However, this tactic often leads to problems later on when the child may not recognize similar or problematic situations in other relationships.

2. **Isolation:** To avoid conflicts or disappointments, some children may choose to isolate themselves, minimizing interaction with the problematic parent. This can manifest as spending a lot of time in their own room, engaging in solitary activities, or avoiding bringing friends home.

3. **Conformity:** Some children become extremely compliant, seeking to please the emotionally immature parent in every possible way. They strive to be the "perfect child," hoping that this will mitigate the parent's problematic behaviors.

4. **Parentification:** Some children may prematurely take on a mature role, trying to take care of their parents or younger siblings. This "reverse parenting" can make the child feel needed and important but can also deprive them of their childhood.

5. **Rebellion:** In contrast to conformity, some children react by rebelling. This rebellion can manifest as defiant behavior, problems at school, or even self-destructive behaviors.

6. **Dissociation:** In particularly traumatic situations, some children may emotionally or mentally "detach" from the situation. They may seem absent or distant, as if their mind is elsewhere. Dissociation is a defense mechanism that helps protect the psyche from unbearable experiences and feelings.

7. **Perfectionism:** Some children seek to control the chaos around them by becoming perfectionists. They strive to get top grades, excel in sports, or other activities, hoping that external success compensates for emotional instability at home.

8. **Developing a Sense of Humor:** Some children use humor as a means of defense. Making jokes or laughing about situations can be a way to lighten the atmosphere and divert attention from the problems.
These coping strategies are ways in which children try to protect themselves and create a sense of normalcy in abnormal situations. However, it's important to note that while they may be helpful in the short term, they can lead to emotional, relational, and behavioral problems in the long term. Awareness of these strategies and understanding the roots of such behaviors are essential for the healing process and for developing healthy relationships in adulthood.

9. Avoidance: In some cases, children may develop an avoidance tendency. This can manifest as avoiding going home after school, spending a lot of time with friends or in extracurricular activities. The goal is often to reduce exposure to the toxic home environment.

10. Building Fantasy Worlds: Especially in younger children, a common strategy for dealing with traumatic situations is the creation of imaginary worlds. These worlds offer refuge from the harsh realities of their lives, allowing them to experience adventures, have imaginary friends, or even assume new identities.

11. Seeking External Role Models: Faced with an inability to connect with an emotionally immature parent, some children may seek alternative role models, such as teachers, coaches, neighbors, or extended family members. These individuals can provide the type of support, guidance, and understanding that is lacking at home.

12. Developing Strong Resilience: Even when raised in adverse environments, many children can develop surprising resilience. They try to find the silver lining in situations, learn from every experience, and seek not to be defeated by adversity.

13. Emotion Suppression: To avoid conflicts or further trauma, some children may choose to suppress their emotions. This may involve not showing sadness, anger, or fear, even when these emotions are clearly present beneath the surface.

14. Hyper-Vigilance: Another common behavior in children growing up in unstable environments is hyper-vigilance. They are constantly alert, looking for signs of danger or changes in their parents' moods. This constant state of alertness can be exhausting and lead to anxiety issues over time.

15. Adoption of Self-Harming Behaviors: In extreme situations, some children may begin to exhibit self-harming behaviors as a way to express their inner suffering or to try to exert some control over their pain.

16. Creation of Family Alliances: In families with more than one child, a dynamic may develop where siblings form alliances to support each other, offering comfort, understanding, and mutual protection.

17. Desire for Escape: Many children and adolescents may cultivate escape fantasies, which can manifest as daydreams about being adopted by another family, running away from home, or, in later years, moving away for college or work as far away as possible from their original family. Every child is unique, and the coping strategies adopted can vary greatly based on the individual's personality and specific family circumstances. However, it's crucial to recognize that these strategies, although often adopted for emotional survival, can have long-term consequences on an individual's mental health and well-being.

18. Imitation of Behaviors: It's not uncommon for children to imitate their parents' behaviors, even if they are harmful. This can manifest as adopting the same limiting beliefs or attitudes or replicating behavioral patterns in the hope of gaining approval or love.

19. Selective Positive Reinforcement: Some children may emphasize or exaggerate rare positive moments with their parents as a means to create a sense of normalcy. This can lead them to remember only the "good" moments, minimizing or completely forgetting the negative episodes.

20. Seeking External Validation: Growing up with parents who do not offer positive affirmations or emotional support, children can become dependent on external approval. This may manifest as social media addiction, a strong need for recognition in academic or athletic activities, or seeking relationships where they constantly feel the need for approval.

21. Development of Problem-Solving Skills: Faced with constant challenges, some children can become particularly adept at problem-solving. This can become a valuable skill that helps them in many areas of life, even though its origin may be rooted in a complicated family context.

22. Formation of Emotional Barriers: To protect themselves from pain or rejection, some children may build emotional walls, making it difficult for others to get close to them or truly understand their feelings.

23. Development of an Obsessive Work Ethic: As a defense mechanism, some children may completely immerse themselves in work or study, seeking to find a sense of worth and fulfillment outside the family sphere.

24. Seeking Refuge in Spirituality or Religion: The quest for comfort and guidance can lead some children toward spirituality or religion. This can provide a sense of belonging and purpose that is missing in their family environment.

25. Excessive Empathy: Interestingly, some children may develop a high level of empathy as a result of their situation. Trying to understand and predict their parents' behaviors, these children can become particularly attuned to the feelings and needs of others, often at the expense of their own needs.

26. Avoidance of Intimacy: Having experienced instability and a lack of emotional support at home, some children may grow up rejecting the idea of intimacy. They may see close relationships as dangerous or unpredictable and, therefore, keep them at a distance.

All of these strategies represent a child's attempts to navigate an uncertain and often painful environment. If not recognized and addressed, many of these tactics can persist into adulthood, influencing relationships, careers, and overall well-being. The key to overcoming these ingrained behaviors is often awareness, education, and, in many cases, professional assistance.

The ability of children to develop coping strategies in response to their upbringing is a testament to both their resilience and vulnerability. Coping strategies are essentially defense mechanisms—learned or innate responses to protect themselves from pain, confusion, and sometimes trauma. But while these strategies can provide temporary relief or a sense of security in times of extreme uncertainty, they can also have negative repercussions.

Within the context of families with emotionally immature parents, these coping strategies often serve as an anchor or lifeline. Children, trying to make sense of their parents' behavior and find ways to navigate an often unpredictable environment, adopt behaviors they believe will help them emotionally survive. Whether it's mimicking learned behaviors, building emotional barriers, or seeking comfort in external activities, the primary goal is often the same: finding stability amidst chaos.

However, the complexity of these coping mechanisms lies in the fact that, while they may offer a kind of temporary refuge, they can also become traps in the long term. For example, a child who develops strong emotional barriers may find themselves, in adulthood, unable to form deep and meaningful relationships. Another who has adopted the habit of constantly seeking external validation may become an adult with low self-esteem and a dependence on the validation of others.

Recognizing and understanding these coping strategies is the crucial first step in addressing them. Once identified, individuals can begin the healing process, which may include therapy, personal reflection, and the development of new, healthier habits and coping strategies. The ultimate goal, of course, is to allow those who grew up in such circumstances to lead a healthy, balanced, and fulfilling adult life, breaking free from the chains of their childhood experiences and building a future based on self-understanding, self-acceptance, and self-love.

8. Self-Rediscovery: Advice on how adults can reconnect with their true selves and passions. Rediscovering oneself after growing up in an environment with emotionally immature parents can be a profound and transformational journey. This rediscovery is not only a response to the need for healing but also represents a path to self-realization and personal balance. Here are some approaches and tips that adults can embrace to reconnect with their true selves and passions:

1. **Introspective Reflection:** Begin by spending time in reflection. This can be done through meditation, journaling, or simply spending time in solitude. Ask yourself, "Who am I really? What are the things I love to do? What are my passions?"
2. **Therapy:** A therapist can help you navigate the complex emotions and challenges that arise from your childhood and provide you with tools and strategies to move forward.
3. **Define Your Values:** Reflect on the values you want to bring into your life and how you wish to live. These values will become your compass, guiding you in your daily decisions.
4. **Try New Activities:** Explore different activities or hobbies you've always wanted to try. This

helps you reconnect with yourself and discover new passions.

5. **Set Boundaries:** Learn to set healthy boundaries with people in your life. This will allow you to protect your emotional and physical space, prioritizing your well-being.

6. **Connect with Nature:** Spend time outdoors. Nature has a special way of helping us reconnect with ourselves and reflect on our place in the world.

7. **Read and Learn:** There are many books and resources available that can assist you in your journey of self-discovery. Seek them out and immerse yourself in readings that resonate with you.

8. **Write a Letter to Your Younger Self:** Writing a letter to your child or teenage self can be a powerful exercise in reflection and healing. Express support, love, and understanding for what you've been through.

9. **Surround Yourself with Positive People:** Create a social environment composed of individuals who support, understand, and encourage you on your journey of self-discovery.

10. **Make Peace with the Past:** Forgiving doesn't mean forgetting or justifying harmful behavior but rather letting go of the burden of old wounds.

11. **Plan and Dream:** Reflect on what you desire for your future and set goals to achieve it. This can include travel, career, relationships, or simply personal experiences you wish to have. Self-rediscovery is a journey that requires time, patience, and dedication. It may involve confronting old wounds and challenges, but the reward is a deeper and more authentic connection with yourself, your passions, and the surrounding world. Through this process, individuals can find a sense of purpose, joy, and fulfillment they may not have known they possessed.

12. **Meditation and Mindfulness:** Practicing meditation and mindfulness can help establish a deeper connection with the present, making it easier to access your inner thoughts and feelings. These practices can also help you detach from old habits and conditioned emotional responses, creating space for new insights and understandings.

13. **Travel and Exploration:** Going to new or unfamiliar places can offer fresh perspectives. These journeys don't necessarily have to be to distant locations; even exploring a new park or neighborhood in your own city can provide new insights.

14. **Participation in Workshops or Retreats:** There are many structured

experiences, such as workshops or retreats, designed specifically to help individuals reconnect with themselves. These can range from yoga retreats to personal growth seminars.

15. Art and Creativity Practices: Expressing yourself through art, whether it's painting, writing, dancing, or making music, can be a powerful tool for self-discovery. Creativity can help channel repressed emotions, giving them shape and expression.

16. Track Your Dreams: Dreams can offer profound insights into your subconscious. Keeping a dream journal can help you identify recurring themes or messages that might provide clues about your true self.

17. Physical Exercise: Moving your body through exercises like yoga, tai chi, or simply walking can help you reconnect with yourself on a physical level, strengthening the mind-body connection.

18. Mindful Nutrition: Paying attention to what you put into your body and how it makes you feel can help you reconnect with yourself. Eating healthy and balanced foods can impact not only your physical health but also your mental and emotional clarity.

19. Spiritual Exploration: Whether you follow a religion, philosophy, or a personal spiritual path, exploring matters of the soul and spirit can offer profound insights into your true self.

12. Volunteering: Helping others can offer a new perspective on yourself and the world around you. Volunteering connects you with people from diverse backgrounds, exposing you to new experiences and helping you assess and reflect on your place in the world.

13. Establish Traditions or Personal Rituals: Creating special moments in your routine, such as reading for an hour every morning, taking an evening walk, or practicing a gratitude ritual, can help you reconnect with yourself in meaningful and mindful ways.

It's important to remember that self-rediscovery is an ongoing journey, not a final destination. Life is constantly evolving, and in the same way, our understanding and connection with ourselves can change and deepen over time. Through this continuous exploration, we can not only learn more about who we truly are but also create a richer and more fulfilling life.

22. Therapy and Counseling: Many adults who grew up with emotionally immature parents can benefit from professional support in navigating their feelings and perceptions. A therapist or counselor can provide an external perspective and tools to address past trauma and anxiety and help establish new behavioral patterns.

23. Support Groups: There are numerous support groups focusing on helping individuals from dysfunctional families. These groups offer a safe environment to share experiences, gain understanding, and build healthy relationships.

24. Reading and Education: There are many literary resources that can provide information and insights into toxic family dynamics and how to overcome them. Reading stories of others who have had similar experiences can offer both comfort and inspiration.

25. Journaling: Regularly writing in a journal can be a powerful form of self-reflection. Putting your thoughts, feelings, and concerns on paper can help process emotions and identify patterns or themes in your life.

26. Relaxation Techniques: Practices like deep breathing, guided visualization, or progressive meditation can help reduce stress and reconnect with your body and mind.

27. Assertiveness Training: Learning to communicate assertively rather than passively or aggressively can help establish healthy boundaries in relationships and express your needs and desires constructively.

28. Stay Informed: Staying up-to-date on research and studies related to personal growth, psychology, and family dynamics can offer new perspectives and methods for reconnecting with yourself.

29. Cultivate Self-Kindness: Many people raised in emotionally immature environments tend to be hard on themselves. Learning to treat yourself with kindness and compassion can be crucial in the self-rediscovery process.

30. Establish New Routines: Breaking old habits and establishing new routines can help build a sense of stability and reconnect with your passions and desires.

31. Exposure to New Experiences: Trying new activities or hobbies can help discover new interests and passions, allowing you to reconnect with parts of yourself that may have been dormant or neglected.

Self-rediscovery is not a linear process. There are ups and downs, and there may be moments of uncertainty or confusion. However, every step forward, no matter how small, is a step toward greater self-understanding and self-acceptance. Self-Rediscovery is a journey undertaken by many individuals who have experienced difficult childhoods or adolescence, especially in the presence of emotionally immature parents. This path, although challenging, is also a powerful opportunity to strengthen one's identity, refine one's worldview, and build a more authentic and fulfilling life.

Methods of Introspection: One of the most important aspects of self-rediscovery is introspection. Through meditation, personal reflection, and journaling, individuals can delve deeply into their past experiences, analyze behavior patterns, and identify areas of growth.

Impact of Relationships: Relationships play a crucial role in self-rediscovery. Whether it's supportive friends, therapists, or mentor figures, the people around us can reflect, challenge, and support our personal growth. Additionally, establishing healthy boundaries in relationships is essential for protecting and nurturing one's growth.

The Power of Vulnerability: Accepting and embracing one's vulnerability can lead to greater authenticity. By acknowledging their fears, insecurities, and scars, individuals can form deeper connections with others and themselves.

Rekindling Lost Passions: Many adults who grew up with emotionally immature parents may have suppressed their passions to adapt or protect themselves. Rediscovering these passions, whether they involve art, sports, writing, or other pursuits, can reignite joy and curiosity in a person's life.

The Path to Self-Acceptance: Self-rediscovery is not just about understanding who you are but also fully accepting yourself, including your flaws and imperfections. Self-acceptance can lead to greater inner peace and the ability to face challenges with resilience and grace.

In conclusion, self-rediscovery following a childhood with emotionally immature parents is not only a means of healing from past wounds but also a way to create a brighter and more authentic future. While the journey may be challenging, it is also filled with discoveries, growth, and transformation. With the right support, resources, and determination, individuals can successfully navigate this path, reconnecting with their true selves and building a life of meaning and fulfillment.

9. **Establishing Boundaries:** Provide tools and strategies for setting healthy boundaries with emotionally immature parents.

Setting Boundaries with Emotionally Immature Parents

The ability to establish healthy boundaries is crucial for anyone looking to build balanced and respectful relationships. For those who grew up with emotionally immature parents, it might be even more critical because they may never have learned how or why such boundaries are necessary. Here's a detailed overview of strategies and tools for establishing these boundaries:

1. **Recognize the Need for Boundaries:** First and foremost, it's essential to recognize and acknowledge your need for boundaries. This may require some introspection and reflection, especially if you grew up in an environment where your needs and desires were often neglected or ignored.

2. **Clearly Define Your Limits:** Understand what makes you feel uncomfortable, stressed, or vulnerable. Whether it's topics of conversation, physical behaviors, or expectations of time spent together, having a clear understanding of what's acceptable for you is fundamental.

3. **Assertive Communication:** The key to establishing effective boundaries is to communicate them clearly and assertively. This means expressing your needs and desires without being aggressive or passive. Assertive communication is direct yet respectful.

4. **Use "I" Instead of "You":** When expressing concerns or setting boundaries, use phrases like "I feel..." or "I need..." instead of pointing fingers

with "You always...". This reduces the likelihood of putting the other person on the defensive.

5. **Be Consistent:** Once boundaries are established, it's essential to be consistent in enforcing them. If you give in every time they are tested, your determination may be taken less seriously in the future.

6. **Prepare Consequences:** If your boundaries are repeatedly ignored, you may need to implement consequences. This could mean limiting time spent with the person or taking breaks from the relationship until your boundaries are respected.

7. **Do Inner Work:** Sometimes, difficulty in setting boundaries may stem from personal insecurities or past traumas. Working with a therapist or counselor can help strengthen your self-esteem and develop the resilience needed to maintain healthy boundaries.

8. **Surround Yourself with Support:** Talk to trusted friends, family members, or therapists about your boundaries and experiences. Having someone who supports you can offer an external perspective and reinforce your determination.

9. **Practice Self-Care:** Establishing boundaries can be emotionally taxing, especially if they are not respected. Make sure to take time for yourself to relax, reflect, and rejuvenate.

Conclusion:

Setting boundaries with emotionally immature parents can be challenging, as they may not recognize or respect these boundaries as others in your life might. However, with determination, clarity, and support, it's possible to create healthy interaction spaces that protect your emotional and physical well-being. While it may take time and patience, and you may need to reaffirm your boundaries multiple times, this effort can ultimately lead to healthier and more respectful relationships, allowing you to live a more authentic and fulfilling life.

Additional Considerations on Boundaries with Emotionally Immature Parents:

Implementing healthy boundaries with emotionally immature parents is a journey that often leads to profound personal realizations and transformations of relational dynamics. Understanding what this entails can aid in the transition:

Dealing with Guilt: One of the primary barriers to creating boundaries is a sense of guilt. There might be a concern that setting boundaries could hurt the feelings of parents or create further tensions. It's essential to remember that safeguarding your well-being is not an act of selfishness but rather a necessity to ensure healthy relationships.

The Dynamic Nature of Boundaries: Boundaries are not always rigid or fixed. They can change over time based on your needs and circumstances. What was an essential boundary at one point may not be so in another, and vice versa.

Parental Response: Emotionally immature parents may react negatively when you attempt to set boundaries. They might minimize, ridicule, or even manipulate to avoid responsibility. In these moments, it's vital to stand firm and remember why these boundaries are necessary.

Utilizing Therapy: Therapy can be an excellent resource for those seeking to establish boundaries with difficult parents. A therapist can offer strategies, support, and a safe environment to explore your concerns and feelings.

Supporting Yourself Through a Support Network: Having friends or other family members who understand and support the desire to establish boundaries can make a significant difference. These allies can provide comfort, advice, and, at times, a helpful external perspective.

The Benefits of Emotional Detachment: In some cases, practicing a certain degree of emotional detachment might be beneficial. This doesn't mean not loving or caring for your parents but rather protecting yourself from potential emotional harm.

Self-Compassion: During this process, it's crucial to practice self-compassion. Establishing boundaries, especially with parental figures, can lead to moments of doubt and inner conflict. Treating yourself with kindness and understanding can help navigate these challenging times.

Reinterpreting the Past: With the establishment of boundaries, old memories or traumas may resurface. This can be an opportunity to reinterpret past events in light of new understanding and growth.

Patience Is Key: Like many other things in life, setting boundaries is a process. There will be ups and downs, successes and challenges. It's important to remember to have patience with yourself and with the process.

In attempting to set boundaries with emotionally immature parents, you may go through a range of emotions, from hope and optimism to frustration and disappointment. However, with commitment and support, it's possible to find a balance that protects personal well-being and provides space for healthier relationships.

**Expectations Towards Emotion
ally Immature Parents:**

When approaching the issue of boundaries, it's essential to assess and possibly recalibrate your expectations towards emotionally immature parents. These parents may struggle to understand or respect others' needs and feelings, making negotiating boundaries potentially challenging.

Identifying Your Own Needs:

Before setting boundaries, it's crucial to recognize and identify your own needs. Ask yourself, "What do I want or need from this relationship?" This reflection can help you clearly outline the boundaries you wish to establish.

Clear and Direct Communication:

Clarity in communication is essential when setting boundaries. This doesn't necessarily mean that emotionally immature parents will understand or accept what is communicated, but it provides the best opportunity to be heard. Using "I" language (e.g., "I feel overwhelmed when you call five times a day") can reduce the likelihood of putting parents on the defensive.

Reinforcing Boundaries:

Once boundaries are established, it may be necessary to reinforce them repeatedly. This can be particularly true if parents have a habit of crossing them or if they are not accustomed to respecting them. Consistency in reinforcement can help establish new dynamics in the relationship.

Self-Examination:

As you work on setting boundaries, it can be helpful to examine your emotional reactions to your parents' behaviors. This self-examination can offer insights into the underlying reasons for your reactions and help formulate more effective strategies for setting and maintaining boundaries.

Avoiding Pitfalls:

It's common for those setting boundaries to feel selfish or bad. However, it's essential to recognize that setting boundaries is an act of self-esteem and self-preservation. It is a fundamental right to establish how you wish to be treated.

Technology and Boundaries:

In the digital age, boundaries are not limited to face-to-face interactions. Establishing online boundaries, such as deciding when and how to respond to messages or calls, can be equally crucial. These digital boundaries can often be more easily controlled through technological means like "Do Not Disturb" settings, filters, and blocking.

Boundaries and Culture:

In some cultures, the idea of setting boundaries with parents may be viewed as disrespectful or incomprehensible. It's crucial to acknowledge the influence of culture on one's approach to boundaries and seek ways to honor your cultural heritage while protecting your well-being.

Flexibility:

While consistency is crucial, sometimes showing a degree of flexibility in boundaries can be beneficial. This flexibility can be particularly important in situations where parents' mental or physical health is at stake or when specific family circumstances arise.

In the process of setting boundaries with emotionally immature parents, the key is to find a balance between respecting your parents and protecting yourself, however complex that may be.

Respect Versus Protection:

In the context of family relationships, there is a subtle line between respecting your parents and protecting yourself. Growing up with emotionally immature parents may have led to a habit of putting aside your needs in favor of your parents'. However, as adults, it's essential to recognize your autonomy and the right to protect your emotional space.

The Importance of Therapy: Many individuals seeking to establish boundaries with emotionally immature parents can find significant support in therapy. A therapist can offer strategies on how to effectively communicate your needs and handle potential conflicts that arise in the process. Additionally, therapy can help unpack past traumas and provide a context for healing.

Seeking External Support: Outside of therapy, it's valuable to seek support from trusted friends, partners, or support groups. These allies can offer an external perspective, encouragement, and advice based on their own cxpcriences.

The Art of Detachment: Sometimes, despite your best efforts, emotionally immature parents may continue to violate established boundaries. In such cases, the art of detachment can become a crucial tool. This doesn't necessarily mean cutting off all contact but rather learning how to interact without getting emotionally entangled in toxic dynamics.

Active Listening: When establishing boundaries, it's also important to practice active listening. This means truly listening to what the parent has to say, even if you disagree. This approach can help reduce misunderstandings and build more effective communication.

Validating Your Feelings: A common challenge for those trying to set boundaries with emotionally immature parents is a tendency to doubt their own feelings or needs. It's essential to remember that your feelings are valid, regardless of how your parents react.

Self-Care: Setting boundaries can be emotionally demanding. Therefore, practicing self-care becomes essential. This may involve taking time for yourself, engaging in hobbies or activities you love, meditating, or any other practice that helps restore balance and inner peace.

Recognizing Your Limitations: In the process of setting boundaries, it's important to recognize that you cannot control your parents' reactions or behaviors. What you can control is how you respond and how you choose to establish and maintain boundaries. Accepting this reality can help reduce frustration and disappointment.

Reflecting on Your Growth: Finally, while facing the challenges that arise in setting boundaries with emotionally immature parents, it can be helpful to reflect on how much you've grown as an individual. Each step, every conversation, and every boundary set is a sign of personal growth and resilience.

Conclusion on Setting Boundaries: Setting boundaries with emotionally immature parents is a intricate journey that embodies both the challenge of confronting past pains and the promise of building a healthier future. When an individual decides to embark on this path, they are seeking to rewrite a script of interaction that may have been in place for decades.

In life, boundaries are essential not only as a defense mechanism but also as a declaration of self-esteem and self-awareness. In the context of parents who may have never demonstrated proper consideration for their child's emotional needs, asserting these boundaries may seem like rebellion. However, at the heart of this "rebellion" is a deep desire for authenticity, respect, and mutual acknowledgment.

The road to establishing these boundaries is not linear. Many may find themselves negotiating, adjusting, or even compromising these boundaries based on circumstances. These variations are not signs of weakness; on the contrary, they are testimonies to the complexity of human relationships and the ongoing evolution of our relationship with ourselves and others.

A notable challenge in creating boundaries is the potential for guilt or obligation that many may feel toward their parents, regardless of the past.

Culture, tradition, and social norms can often exacerbate these feelings, imposing expectations of a child's "duty" to their parents. However, it's essential to recognize that an individual's first duty is to themselves and their well-being. Over time, and often with the support of therapy or counseling, a person can come to see these boundaries not as barriers but as bridges to a healthier, more balanced type of relationship. Ultimately, setting boundaries is not an act of separation but an aspiration to clarity, understanding, and harmony. Through this process, one reaffirms their identity, values their intrinsic worth, and builds a solid foundation for future relationships based on mutual respect and genuine care.

10.   **Managing Anger and Resentment:**

Provide techniques for managing and processing these emotions in a healthy way.

Managing Anger and Resentment: Anger and resentment are natural emotional reactions that can emerge when reflecting on the past, especially in the presence of emotionally immature parents. These feelings, if not addressed properly, can lead to a cycle of negativity, adversely affecting overall well-being and interpersonal relationships.

1. **Acknowledging Feelings:** The first step in managing anger and resentment is acknowledging them. Ignoring or suppressing these feelings can lead to an accumulation of negative emotions that may explode unexpectedly. Accepting that it's normal to feel angry or resentful allows you to begin the processing.

2. **Healthy Expression of Anger:** Expressing anger in a healthy way can prevent the buildup of tensions. This can include techniques such as journaling, engaging in sports or martial arts, or talking to a trusted friend or therapist.

3. **Relaxation Techniques:** Practices like meditation, yoga, and deep breathing can help calm the mind and reduce anger. These techniques help bring awareness to the present moment, diverting attention from negative thoughts.

4. **Therapy and Counseling:** Talking to a therapist or counselor can offer an external perspective and specific tools for managing and processing anger and resentment. This type of support can help better understand the roots of these feelings and find effective ways to address them.

5. **Reevaluating Expectations:** Often, anger and resentment can arise from unmet expectations. Reevaluating these expectations and accepting that everyone, including parents, is human and has limitations, can help release the burden of unrealistic expectations.

6. **Forgiveness as Liberation:** Forgiveness doesn't mean forgetting or justifying harmful behavior. Instead, it's an act of personal liberation from the weight of anger and resentment. Forgiveness may take time and may not be appropriate in all situations, but it can offer a profound sense of peace and freedom.

7. **Limiting Exposure:** If interacting with emotionally immature parents continues to evoke feelings of anger or resentment, it may be helpful to limit exposure to these interactions. Establishing healthy boundaries can assist in this process.

Conclusion: Managing anger and resentment is a journey that requires commitment, awareness, and often external support. It's essential to remember that these feelings are valid and deserve to be treated with care and consideration. Through self-awareness, reflection, and practice, it's possible to find ways to process these emotions healthily, creating space for healing, growth, and healthier relationships in the future.

Managing Anger and Resentment: Some may argue that anger and resentment, when managed correctly, can actually provide valuable insights. These feelings might signal where there have been wounds and where further growth or understanding may be needed. They can also serve as catalysts for change and self-transcendence.

Creative Methods for Processing Anger:

- **Art as an Outlet:** Painting, drawing, or sculpting can help transfer intense emotions onto a canvas or a piece of clay. Transforming the energy of anger into a work of art can be an effective way to see your anger from a new perspcctive and process it.

- **Music and Anger:** Listening to, writing, or playing music can be another way to express and process anger. Music has the power to reach deep into the soul and resonate with our innermost emotions.

Rethinking Our Story:

- **Narrative Rewriting:** Reconsidering past events and rewriting your own story can be a powerful way to reconfigure the meaning of certain experiences. This doesn't mean denying or minimizing trauma but rather seeking a new meaning or perspective on events.

Introspective Reflection Techniques:

- **Loving-Kindness Meditation (Metta):** This form of meditation aims to cultivate feelings of love and compassion for oneself and others. It can help neutralize resentment and anger, replacing them with understanding and empathy.
- **Journaling:** Keeping a journal of your emotions can provide insights into what triggers your anger. Writing can also help release these emotions constructively.

Cognitive Techniques: Cognitive Distortions: Recognizing and challenging cognitive distortions can help see situations from a more objective perspective. For instance, acknowledging when you are generalizing a situation or taking things too personally can help reduce anger. Addressing Unrealistic Expectations: Recognizing when you expect too much from yourself or others and adjusting these expectations can help reduce frustration and anger. Nonviolent Communication: This technique focuses on understanding and expressing one's needs constructively, without attacking or blaming others. Practicing Gratitude: Even amid anger, finding moments or aspects of life to be grateful for can help balance negative emotions and offer a more balanced perspective.

In essence, recognizing and accepting anger and resentment as part of the human emotional repertoire is the first step. However, it is equally crucial to find healthy and constructive methods to express and process these feelings, preventing them from taking over and negatively affecting our daily lives.

Managing Anger and Resentment: Anger and resentment, especially when linked to trauma or childhood experiences, are complex and powerful emotions that can deeply influence our psyche and relationships. Growing up in an environment with emotionally immature parents may mean that these emotions were often suppressed, unrecognized, or directed in unhealthy ways.

The Physical Impact of Anger and Resentment: Our body physically reacts to these feelings. It can increase heart rate, blood pressure, and adrenaline levels. Long-term, if not managed correctly, these states can lead to health issues such as heart disease, immune system problems, and insomnia.

Connecting with Your Emotions: Before effectively managing anger, it's important to recognize it. This may require a deep dive into emotions and reflection on what you actually feel. Mindfulness practices, like mindfulness itself, can help become more aware of your emotional responses.

The Effects of Past Experiences: Individuals raised with emotionally immature parents may have developed a sense of repressed anger due to neglected needs or violated boundaries during childhood. This repressed anger can manifest in various ways, such as passive-aggressive behavior, explosive anger, or self-destructive tendencies.

Breathing and Grounding Techniques: When anger is felt, returning to the present moment can help manage it. Techniques such as deep breathing or grounding exercises, like focusing on your senses or holding an object, can help bring the mind back to the present moment and divert it from the source of anger.

Seeking External Support: Sometimes, dealing with anger and resentment, especially if rooted in deep trauma, may require the help of a professional. A therapist or counselor can provide specific tools and techniques to process these emotions and find paths to healing.

Addressing Anger Triggers: Identifying what triggers anger can be a fundamental step in its management. Once these triggers are identified, you can work to avoid such situations or develop healthier strategies to handle them.

Learning to Respond, Not React: A fundamental concept in anger management is the ability to respond rather than impulsively react. This means taking a moment to reflect on the situation and consciously decide how to act, rather than letting automatic reactions take over.

Anger and resentment are natural emotions, but the key is to learn to manage them so they don't dominate our lives or relationships. Through awareness, understanding, and the adoption of effective strategies, it's possible to live a more balanced and peaceful life.

Conclusion on Managing Anger and Resentment: Managing anger and resentment is not just about immediate emotional control; it's a profound journey of self-understanding, acceptance, and transformation. These feelings, when rooted in childhood experiences with emotionally immature parents, carry complex layers of pain, disappointments, and unmet expectations. In adulthood, these emotions can manifest in many ways: through relationship issues, difficulties in social interactions, work-related problems, and even health issues. What often starts as a childhood-related reaction can easily become an ingrained behavioral pattern that influences all areas of life. Adults experiencing such feelings often struggle to identify them as connected to their past experiences. They may perceive their anger as a reaction to current circumstances, ignoring the historical depth of these emotions. The ability to connect with these roots can offer insight and understanding, providing a foundation for more effective management and healing. It's also important to recognize that while anger and resentment are often viewed negatively, they also serve as indications of our inner need for acknowledgment, understanding, and change. With the right support and adequate tools, these emotions can become catalysts for profound personal growth and transformation.

11. Rebuilding Relationships with Emotionally Immature Parents: Embarking on the journey of rebuilding or renegotiating relationships with emotionally immature parents can be one of the most challenging yet rewarding tasks. It requires deep introspection, understanding, and sometimes even the ability to set aside one's ego for the sake of the relationship. Here are some guidelines to navigate this path:

1. **Self-Understanding and Emotional Preparation:** Before attempting to rebuild a relationship, it's essential to have a clear understanding of your own feelings, expectations, and boundaries. Through therapy, meditation, or other forms of introspection, you can come to understand your wounds and what

you want to achieve through renegotiating the relationship.

2. **Effective Communication:** Talking to emotionally immature parents often requires a different type of communication. Using nonviolent communication, which emphasizes expressing your feelings and needs without assigning blame, can be particularly effective.

3. **Setting Clear Boundaries:** Deciding in advance what your limits are and communicating them clearly is fundamental. This may include how much time you're willing to spend with your parents, which topics you're willing to discuss, and how you want to be treated.

4. **Letting Go of Expectations:** Even though you may hope for your parents to change or evolve, rigidly clinging to this expectation can lead to further disappointments. Recognizing that they may not change and deciding how you want to manage the relationship based on that is crucial.

5. **Seeking Mediation or Family Therapy:** In some cases, having an impartial third party to facilitate communication and assist in renegotiating the relationship can be helpful.

6. **Self-Protection:** While seeking to renegotiate or rebuild a relationship, it's vital to ensure you protect your mental and emotional well-being. This may involve limiting the time spent with

your parents, seeking external support, or taking breaks when necessary.

7. **Practice Forgiveness:** Forgiveness doesn't necessarily mean reconciliation or forgetting. It may simply involve releasing the burden of resentment for your own well-being. This can take time and may not come immediately, but it can be a crucial step in the healing process.

8. **Acknowledging Small Victories:** Rebuilding relationships is a process, and there will be ups and downs. Celebrating small progress can help maintain a positive outlook and recognize personal growth that is occurring.

In conclusion, rebuilding or renegotiating a relationship with emotionally immature parents can be a long and winding journey. However, with the right preparation, tools, and support, it is possible to find a new dynamic that honors both your needs and those of your parents. While every situation is unique, approaching it with compassion, understanding, and clarity can offer the best opportunity for a renewed and healthy relationship.

Rebuilding or renegotiating a relationship with emotionally immature parents can often feel like walking on unstable ground. Family dynamics can be rooted in years, if not decades, of behavioral patterns and expectations.

Here are additional reflections and considerations on the topic:

Mixed Emotions: It can be common to experience a range of emotions when interacting with emotionally immature parents. There may be love but also anger, sadness, confusion, and sometimes hope. Recognizing and accepting that you can love someone but not necessarily love their behavior is a fundamental step in the process.

Memory and Perception: Your childhood memories and current perceptions may differ from those of your parents. There may be inaccuracies in their perception of past events or in your expectations. Understanding these differences in perception can aid in communication and mutual understanding.

The Importance of Active Listening: When approaching emotionally immature parents, active listening can become a crucial tool. Active listening, which means fully focusing on what the other person is saying, can help better understand their perspective and build bridges of understanding.

Authenticity vs. Protection: While it's crucial to remain authentic in your feelings and needs, it may also be necessary to protect yourself from further emotional harm. This may mean not sharing every detail of your feelings or experiences, especially if you believe they might be minimized or ridiculed.

Incremental Reconstruction: Rebuilding a relationship doesn't necessarily mean returning to complete intimacy or openness immediately. It can start with small gestures or conversations, slowly building trust over time.

The Challenge of Vulnerability: Being vulnerable, especially with those who have hurt us in the past, can be extremely difficult. However, vulnerability can also open the door to a deeper and more meaningful connection. Carefully consider when and how to show your vulnerability, ensuring it happens in a safe and supportive environment.

Future Expectations: While working to rebuild a relationship, it can also be helpful to imagine what you want the relationship to be like in the future. This can help guide actions and decisions as you navigate the process. Recognizing the challenges that can arise when trying to rebuild a relationship with emotionally immature parents is crucial. Every step forward, no matter how small, is a step in the right direction. And while the journey may be filled with difficulties, the rewards of a renewed and improved relationship can be immeasurable.

The Role of Family Therapy: Family therapy can provide a neutral and professional space where parents and children can explore problematic relational dynamics. A qualified therapist can help mediate conversations, offering insights and tools to improve communication and resolve conflicts.

Setting Time Boundaries: There may be times when you need to take a break from interacting with your parents to protect your mental and emotional health. Defining a period of "pause" can give both parties time to reflect and recover.

Mutual Respect: Even if you feel hurt by your parents' behaviors, recognizing and respecting their individuality and life experiences can pave the way for greater empathy on both sides. This doesn't mean justifying toxic behavior but rather seeking to understand where it's coming from.

Establishing Relational Priorities: Identify which aspects of the relationship matter most to you. You may decide you want to work on trust, communication, or intimacy first. Having clear priorities can help guide the rebuilding process.

Taking Responsibility for Your Actions: If you find yourself in a position where you can do so, taking responsibility for your own actions or words that may have contributed to conflicts can send a signal to your parents that you're serious about making positive changes in the relationship.

Celebrate Small Successes: Rebuilding a relationship takes time and patience. Every small success, such as a productive conversation or a mutual gesture of affection, deserves recognition and celebration.

Recognizing the Power of Forgiveness: Forgiveness doesn't mean forgetting or minimizing past hurts. It means freeing yourself from the weight of those memories and emotions so you can move forward. Consider whether you're ready to forgive and what it means to you.

Building New Traditions: Once the relationship begins to stabilize, you might consider the idea of creating new traditions with your parents. This can help replace old painful memories with new positive moments.

Flexibility in the Process: Every relationship is unique, and what works for one person may not work for another. Being flexible in your approach to rebuilding the relationship and willing to try different strategies can be crucial.

External Resources and Support: Don't underestimate the power of external support. Support groups, books, seminars, and courses can offer valuable tools and different perspectives on navigating these complex waters.

Rebuilding relationships, especially those with such deep and complex roots as those between parents and children, is no small task. It's an intricate journey, filled with emotions ranging from hope to disappointment, from anger to acceptance. But the reason many people choose to embark on this path is the intrinsic belief that, beyond the wounds of the past, there exists an authentic connection worth saving and nurturing.

The first step on this rebuilding journey is understanding. Understanding that the actions and behaviors of emotionally immature parents are often the result of their own unresolved wounds and inner conflicts. This understanding doesn't justify their harmful behaviors but can help reframe the situation in a different light, offering a foundation of empathy to start from. Taking responsibility for your own actions is essential but must be balanced with the expectation that the other party should do the same. Without reciprocity in this process, rebuilding may not be sustainable in the long term. Every small success along the way should be seen as a signal that the hard work is paying off. But it's also essential to prepare for possible setbacks. Relationships are dynamic and can have highs and lows.

Forgiveness emerges as one of the most challenging yet liberating aspects of the process. Forgiving doesn't mean forgetting, nor does it mean accepting similar future behaviors. Instead, it means freeing oneself from the burden of bitterness and making room for healing. And while forgiveness is a gift to oneself, establishing healthy boundaries ensures that one can move forward without compromising their well-being. Building new traditions and creating new positive memories can transform a strained relationship into one that is a source of joy and satisfaction. This doesn't erase the challenges of the past but helps balance them with positive experiences, creating a brighter and more balanced future for both parties.

Lastly, the importance of external support cannot be emphasized enough. Whether it's therapy, support groups, or simply trusted friends, having a support network can make the difference between feeling alone on this journey and feeling supported and understood.

In conclusion, rebuilding a relationship with emotionally immature parents is a challenging but potentially rewarding journey. It requires time, patience, understanding, and, above all, the willingness of both parties to engage in the process. With the right resources and mindset, it's possible to find middle ground and build a deeper and more meaningful connection.

Therapeutic Support: Promoting the Importance of Therapy and How It Can Aid in Healing

Therapeutic Support: Therapy is a collaborative process between an individual and a qualified professional with the goal of addressing and resolving emotional, psychological, or behavioral issues. For those who have faced challenges stemming from being raised by emotionally immature parents, therapeutic support can offer numerous benefits in the healing journey.

1. **Safe Environment:** Therapy provides a safe and confidential environment where the individual can freely express their feelings, fears, and concerns without the fear of judgment or misunderstanding.

2. **Deep Understanding:** Through therapy, individuals can gain a deeper understanding of the roots of their problems. With the help of a therapist, they can examine family dynamics and identify inherited behavioral patterns.

3. **Tools and Strategies:** A therapist can provide tools and strategies to address specific emotional or behavioral issues. This may include stress management techniques, ways to establish

healthy boundaries, or strategies to improve communication skills.

4. **Validation:** For many people, feeling seen and understood is a fundamental aspect of healing. A therapist can offer valid validation of the individual's experiences, helping reaffirm their reality.

5. **Healing Process:** Therapy doesn't offer quick fixes but can guide individuals through a structured process of introspection, confrontation, and resolution. This journey can help address past traumas and build a foundation for a healthier and more fulfilling future.

6. **Support in Confrontation:** For those who choose to confront their parents or other significant figures, a therapist can offer support, preparation, and guidance in the process.

7. **Self-Exploration:** In addition to exploring past wounds, therapy can also offer the opportunity to explore one's self, aspirations, values, and desires, enabling personal growth and greater self-awareness.

8. **Support Network:** Often, a therapist can recommend support groups or other resources that can aid in the healing journey. These groups can provide a sense of community and the awareness that one is not alone in their experience.

In conclusion, therapeutic support is an essential component for many in their healing journey from traumas related to being raised by emotionally immature parents. It offers a combination of professional listening, insight, practical tools, and a safe and supportive environment to navigate the complex territory of emotional wounds and embark on a journey toward well-being. Each individual is unique, and therapy can be tailored to meet specific needs and circumstances.

Types of Therapies and Their Benefits: Various forms of therapy offer a wide range of approaches and methodologies to address issues stemming from childhood with emotionally immature parents.

1. **Cognitive-Behavioral Therapy (CBT):** This therapy focuses on how thoughts influence behaviors and emotions. It is particularly effective for addressing negative or distorted thought patterns. For example, an individual may have developed the belief that they are unworthy of love due to their parents' behavior; through CBT, they can learn to challenge and change this thought pattern.

2. **Psychodynamic Therapy:** Based on the idea that childhood experiences influence adult personality and behavior, it explores how past

traumas or relationships affect present relationships and behaviors.

3. **Person-Centered Therapy:** This therapy emphasizes creating an atmosphere of acceptance and understanding, allowing the individual to explore their feelings in a safe space.

4. **Family Therapy:** Useful for adults looking to address family dynamics with their parents or other family members, this approach considers the family as a unit and seeks to resolve conflicts and improve communication within it.

5. **Art Therapy:** Art can serve as a vehicle for expressing emotions and traumas that may be difficult to verbalize. Drawing, painting, or sculpting can help reveal and process repressed feelings.

6. **Body-Based Therapy:** Since trauma can be stored in the body, techniques such as dance therapy or movement-based therapy can be helpful in releasing blocked emotions and working through physical and emotional traumas.

7. **Mindfulness and Mindfulness-Based Therapies:** These practices help individuals connect with the present, reduce anxiety, and become more aware of their thought patterns and reactions.

8. **Support Groups:** While not a formal form of therapy, support groups provide an environment where individuals can share their experiences and find solidarity with others who have had similar experiences.

Every individual has unique needs, and what works for one person may not work for another. It may be necessary to try different types of therapy or combine multiple approaches to find what is most effective. However, the common factor in every form of therapy is the opportunity to explore and process emotions in a safe and supportive space. The key is to find a therapist or approach that one feels comfortable with and that meets the individual's specific needs.

Therapy as a Tool for Empowerment and Self-Understanding: Many adults who grew up with emotionally immature parents may have developed a range of defense mechanisms and coping strategies that, while useful during childhood, can become obstacles in adulthood. Therapy can serve as a space where these mechanisms can be recognized, understood, and reworked.

Rebuilding Self-Esteem: One of the most significant damages caused by being raised by emotionally immature parents is low self-esteem. Many may feel as if they are not "good enough" or struggle with a pervasive sense of shame.

Therapy can help uproot these false beliefs and build a sense of worth and self-esteem.

Healing from Trauma: Not everyone raised by emotionally immature parents experiences trauma in the traditional sense, but many have gone through traumatic episodes or prolonged stress. Therapy can provide tools and resources to address and heal from these traumatic experiences.

Relaxation and Stress Reduction Techniques: Therapy can also provide a range of techniques for managing stress, such as deep breathing, meditation, or guided visualization. These techniques can be particularly helpful for those who have developed anxious or hyperactive responses as a result of their childhood experiences.

Reconstructing Personal Narrative: The story we tell ourselves about our childhood and identity can have a profound impact on how we see ourselves and relate to others. Therapy can help individuals rewrite these narratives in ways that are more truthful and empowering.

Strategies for Building Healthy Relationships: After living with emotionally immature parents, it can be challenging to know what constitutes a healthy relationship. Through therapy, individuals can learn what it means to have a balanced relationship and how to build healthy bonds with others.

Understanding the Generational Cycle: It is crucial to understand that, if left unaddressed, behavior patterns can pass from generation to generation. Therapy can help individuals recognize these patterns and make conscious decisions about how they want to interact with their children or other family members.

In summary, while childhood wounds can leave deep scars, therapy offers a path to healing and transformation. It's not just about "talking about one's problems" but using tools, resources, and insights to create a happier, healthier, and more fulfilling life.

Conclusion on Therapeutic Support: Therapy serves as a beacon in the journey of self-understanding and healing for those who have faced the challenges of being raised by emotionally immature parents. This form of professional intervention goes beyond providing a safe place to express pain and trauma; it offers readily applicable tools and transformative insights that can change the course of an individual's life.

The Importance of Personalization: There is no one-size-fits-all therapeutic approach. Every individual carries a unique story, and therefore, it is essential for the therapist to tailor their approach to the patient's specific needs. This customization ensures that the treatment is as effective as possible and addresses the individual challenges each patient presents. **Empowerment through Understanding:** One of the fundamental goals of therapy is to enable the individual to understand the roots of their behaviors, emotions, and thought patterns. This understanding can provide a sense of control as the person begins to recognize that they are not "flawed" but that their reactions and behaviors are often the result of past experiences. **Therapy as a Long-Term Commitment:** While some people may benefit from a few therapy sessions, many find that deep healing takes time. The therapeutic journey is not a linear path, and there may be a mix of progress and challenging moments. It is essential to recognize that persistence in the process can lead to lasting transformation.

The Power of Connection: Beyond specific techniques and tools, one of the most healing aspects of therapy is the relationship between the therapist and the patient. Feeling seen, heard, and understood can be incredibly powerful, especially for those who did not have these experiences during childhood.

Ultimately, the decision to seek therapeutic support is an act of courage and an investment in one's future well-being. For many, it represents the first significant step toward creating a richer, more satisfying life free from the burdens of the past. As such, therapy should not be seen as a sign of weakness but rather as a recognition of one's strength and determination to live a better life.

Case Stories: Sharing Real-Life Examples of Individuals Who Faced and Overcame the Challenges of Having Emotionally Immature Parents.

Case Story 1: Marco and the Quest for Autonomy Marco grew up in a family where his mother had the habit of making decisions for him. Even small choices, such as what clothes to wear or which friends to hang out with, were often decided by his mother. As an adult, Marco realized he had difficulty making independent decisions and trusting his judgment. Through therapy, he learned to recognize and challenge these learned patterns and gradually gained more independence in his life.

Case Story 2: Clara and the Quest for Acceptance Clara grew up often feeling rejected by her father, an emotionally distant man. Every time she tried to get closer or share her feelings, he would push her away or minimize her emotions. As an adult, Clara constantly sought approval and acceptance in her relationships. With the help of therapy, she began to understand the origins of this pattern and worked to find acceptance and self-love, reducing her dependence on external approval.

Case Story 3: Paolo and the Fear of Expression Raised in an environment where emotions were never discussed or validated, Paolo had learned to suppress his feelings and avoid conflicts. This pattern influenced his adult relationships, where he often found himself sacrificing his own needs to maintain peace. Through therapy, Paolo learned the importance of expressing his feelings and needs and developed communication skills that allowed him to have more balanced and satisfying relationships.

Case Story 4: Silvia and Resilience Silvia was often ridiculed and belittled by her mother during her childhood. This led her to develop low self-esteem and difficulty trusting others. However, she also developed strong resilience. As an adult, Silvia sought therapeutic support and discovered the inner strength she had built as a defense mechanism. She used this resilience to confront her past traumas and build a happy and fulfilled life. These examples illustrate how, despite the challenges of having emotionally immature parents, individuals can find paths to healing and transformation. Through awareness, support, and determination, it is possible to overcome learned patterns and create a life of satisfaction and well-being.

Case Story 5: Beatrice and the Power of Forgiveness Beatrice grew up in an environment where silences were more eloquent than words. Her emotionally immature father often avoided confrontation and ignored his daughter's emotional needs. This behavior left Beatrice with a deep sense of being unseen or unrecognized. As an adult, she carried repressed anger and a profound sense of injustice. However, through support group meetings and therapy, she learned the art of forgiveness. It wasn't about excusing her father's behavior but freeing herself from the weight of those painful memories.

Case Story 6: Roberto and Learning Vulnerability Due to frequent criticism and judgment from his father, Roberto had built a wall around his true feelings, showing only a mask of confidence to the outside world. This defense, while protecting him during childhood, had become a prison in his adulthood. He had difficulty establishing deep connections with others and feared vulnerability. With the help of an experienced therapist, Roberto gradually learned to break down that wall, discovering that showing his vulnerability could lead to deeper and more meaningful relationships.

Case Story 7: Giulia and the Rediscovery of Self-Esteem Giulia had always felt that she didn't live up to her mother's expectations, a demanding and often dissatisfied woman. This led her to constantly doubt herself and her abilities. However, as an adult, a series of positive experiences at work and meaningful encounters with loving friends began to challenge this negative self-image. Giulia embarked on a journey of self-discovery, recognizing her self-worth and learning how to nurture and protect her self-esteem.

Case Story 8: Lorenzo and the Support Network Growing up with emotionally distant parents, Lorenzo always felt alone. This loneliness influenced his youth and early adulthood, often leading him to isolate himself. However, a series of circumstances led him to join a support group for people with similar family stories. This support network became crucial for him, offering not only understanding and shared experiences but also tools and resources to address and overcome past wounds. These stories emphasize the resilience of the human spirit, demonstrating that, despite a difficult childhood, with the right resources and support, it is possible to find a path to healing and reconciliation with the past.

Case Story 9: Chiara and the Art of Meditation Chiara grew up in a chaotic environment, with emotionally unstable parents who rarely provided a stable anchor. As an adult, anxiety and stress seemed to be her constant companions. One day, however, she was introduced to meditation by a friend. Through daily practice, Chiara discovered an oasis of inner peace that allowed her to detach from the scars of her past and live in the present. Meditation became her anchor, enabling her to navigate life's challenges with greater calmness and centeredness.

Case Story 10: Fabio and the Power of Journaling For Fabio, writing had always been an enjoyable activity, but he had never considered using it as a tool for introspection and healing. Raised with critical and often disparaging parents, he had developed a negative self-image. Starting to write a journal became a way for him to express, process, and ultimately release these repressive emotions. Over time, through the pages of his journal, Fabio gained a deeper understanding of himself and built a more balanced and compassionate view of his personal history.

Case Story 11: Elena and Exploration Through Travel Elena had always felt an overwhelming sense of being "trapped" in her hometown, bound by painful memories of a childhood spent with emotionally immature parents. So, as soon as she had the opportunity, she decided to embark on a solo journey through different countries. Each new place, culture, and encounter became a step in her journey of self-discovery. Far from being a mere escape, the journey became a way for Elena to confront herself, recognizing that, despite her past, she had the power to define her future.

Case Story 12: Marco and Connection with Nature Nature had always held a special fascination for Marco. Raised in an urban environment with emotionally absent parents, he found solace in occasional countryside hikes or visits to parks. As an adult, he made the decision to move to a more rural area, surrounding himself with the tranquility and serenity of nature. This change not only offered him a respite from the hustle and bustle of city life but also became a powerful catalyst for his emotional healing. Surrounded by nature, Marco learned the importance of release, renewal, and regeneration, concepts he also applied to his inner life.

Case Story 13: Valentina and the Art of Dance Valentina had always felt a strong connection to music since childhood, but she never had the opportunity to express her love for it due to a rigid and unsupportive family environment. As an adult, she decided to enroll in contemporary dance classes. She soon discovered that dance was not only a way to move her body but also a powerful means of emotional expression. Through her movements, Valentina began to release old traumas and fears, and she reestablished a connection with herself that she had lost. Dance became her outlet, a safe place to freely express her emotions.

Case Story 14: Luca and Animal Therapy
From a young age, Luca had always had a special bond with animals. In a childhood marked by misunderstanding and a lack of emotional support, moments spent with his dog provided him with a safe haven. As an adult, he decided to utilize animal-assisted therapy. Interacting with horses, dogs, and other animals became a way for him to rediscover a genuine and non-judgmental connection. He found that through contact with these beings, he could break down emotional walls and embark on a journey of authentic healing.

Case Story 15: Arianna and Cooking as Therapy Arianna had always had a complicated relationship with food due to family dynamics. However, as an adult, she came across a book on mindful cooking and decided to experiment with preparing dishes consciously. She discovered that cooking could become a therapeutic experience: every ingredient, every step of the preparation, became an act of presence and care. Cooking became a ritual for Arianna, a moment to express creativity and love, and a way to rediscover the genuine pleasure of nourishing oneself in every sense.

Case Story 16: Matteo and Climbing Matteo had spent much of his childhood feeling "stuck," both physically and emotionally, due to family dynamics. Once he grew up, a friend introduced him to rock climbing. Initially skeptical, he soon realized that climbing was not just a physical activity but also an inner journey. Every mountain, every wall, represented a challenge, an opportunity to overcome fears and limitations. Through climbing, Matteo learned the importance of determination, resilience, and self-confidence, regaining a sense of freedom he had lost.

In conclusion, the stories of individuals who have faced challenges stemming from a childhood with emotionally immature parents underscore how each person can find personalized and unique paths to healing and self-discovery. While childhood and family environment play a crucial role in character formation and relational dynamics, the human capacity for resilience and rebirth is remarkably powerful.

People like Valentina, Luca, Arianna, and Matteo represent a sample of the countless ways individuals can overcome past wounds and rediscover their authenticity. Each story, though unique, carries common traits: the search for a deep connection with oneself, the desire to express and release repressed emotions, and the need to find an outlet or anchor in the external world.

Healing modalities vary widely: while some individuals may find comfort and catharsis in art and creativity, as Valentina and Arianna did, others may discover therapy through contact with nature or animals, as Luca and Matteo did. These stories testify that healing does not have a fixed formula but adapts to the needs and desires of each person.

It's also crucial to recognize the importance of the environment and the people surrounding the individual during their healing journey. Friends, therapists, mentors, or even strangers who cross their path can offer support, understanding, and guidance toward self-discovery. These stories are a testament to the power of the human being to regenerate, reinvent, and find new meanings, regardless of the adversities faced in the past.

15. The Importance of Self-Care

Self-care is not a superficial concept or a luxury reserved for a few; it's a fundamental necessity to maintain mental, physical, and emotional balance. Just as we take care of our physical needs by eating, drinking water, and sleeping, we must also take care of our emotional and psychological needs.

1. **Listen to Your Body:** Often, our bodies send clear signals about what they need. Fatigue, irritability, and headaches can be symptoms of stress or unmet needs. Take time to rest and recharge when needed.

2. **Set Boundaries:** This means recognizing when to say "no" to others' requests and establishing clear boundaries to protect your time, energy, and well-being.

3. **Connect with Nature:** Spending time outdoors, walking in a park, hiking, or simply sitting under a tree can have a calming and rejuvenating effect.

4. **Practice Mindfulness:** Meditation, mindful breathing, and other mindfulness techniques can help you stay anchored in the present, reducing anxiety and stress.

5. **Physical Exercise:** Physical activity not only keeps the body fit but also releases endorphins, natural chemicals that promote well-being and reduce stress.

6. **Express Yourself:** Whether it's writing, painting, dancing, cooking, or any other form of expression, allow yourself to unleash your creativity and emotions.

7. **Connect with Others:** Human connection is essential. Talking to friends, sharing moments with family, or even making new acquaintances can help you feel supported and understood.

8. **Establish a Routine:** Having a daily routine, even a flexible one, can provide a sense of structure and predictability amid chaos.

9. **Continuous Learning:** Learning something new, whether it's a hobby, a language, or any other skill, can provide a sense of accomplishment and purpose.

10. **Seek Professional Support:** Sometimes, challenges can become too overwhelming to face alone. Therapists, counselors, and coaches can provide valuable tools and perspectives.

In conclusion, self-care is not a selfish act. It is a commitment to one's own health and well-being. When dealing with life's challenges, especially those related to emotionally immature parents, self-care becomes even more crucial. Through daily practices and a deep awareness of your needs, every individual can build a solid foundation to face life's challenges with resilience and strength.

The topic of self-care is truly vast and crucial. Over time, many people have come to realize that self-attention is not a sign of selfishness but rather a form of respect and love for oneself, which is then reflected in all external interactions. Here are some further insights on the subject:

Self-care is intrinsically linked to the concept of self-esteem. When we recognize our worth, we naturally tend to take care of ourselves. Conversely, if we don't see ourselves as deserving of attention and care, it's easy to neglect ourselves. The key lies in building a healthy relationship with oneself, often starting with small daily acts.

Another crucial aspect of self-care is the ability to recognize and listen to our own emotions. Many of us have been taught to suppress certain emotions, especially those considered "negative." However, self-care requires that we make space for all our emotions, accepting them as part of our being. When we feel sadness, anger, or frustration, self-care might mean taking a moment to reflect on what we're feeling, rather than ignoring or stifling those emotions.

The environment we live in plays a fundamental role in our well-being. Self-care can also mean creating a space that makes us feel safe, peaceful, and comfortable. Whether it's a well-decorated home, a meditation room, or a reading nook, having a personal space to retreat to and relax is crucial.

Nutrition is another pillar of self-care. Nourishing the body with healthy and nutritious foods, drinking plenty of water, and reducing or avoiding substances that can harm our well-being (such as excessive alcohol, caffeine, or refined sugars) are all actions that reflect a deep care for oneself.

Lastly, self-care doesn't mean isolating oneself from the world. On the contrary, it often involves actively seeking out communities and support groups that share similar interests or challenges. Being part of a community can provide a sense of belonging and support that is crucial for our psychological well-being.

All these aspects are tightly interconnected and contribute to an overall framework of health and well-being. The key is balance: recognizing what is needed at any given moment and acting accordingly, without judgment and with kindness toward oneself. The path to self-care is an ongoing journey, filled with discoveries, challenges, and moments of growth.

Self-care is not limited to just physical practices or dietary habits; it also encompasses mental and spiritual health. Our psyche is just as important as our physical body and requires regular attention to ensure its well-being.

One facet of mental self-care involves stress management. We live in a world where demands and pressures are constant, coming from both external and internal sources. Finding effective ways to manage stress, such as meditation, writing, or simply spending time in nature, can have profoundly positive effects on our mental health.

The practice of mindfulness, or awareness, has become increasingly popular as a self-care tool. By focusing on the present moment and accepting it without judgment, you can attain a form of inner peace and mental clarity that might otherwise be hard to find.

Furthermore, dedicating time to your passions and hobbies is not only a way to relax but also to recharge and reignite your inner spark. Whether it's painting, dancing, reading, or any other activity that resonates with your soul, it's crucial to carve out time for these passions.

Another often overlooked aspect of self-care is the quality of sleep. Adequate sleep is essential for our physical and mental health. This involves creating a conducive environment for rest, having an evening routine that signals to your body it's time to wind down, and, if necessary, using relaxation techniques to aid in falling asleep.

Self-care also encompasses the importance of setting boundaries. This means recognizing when you need a break and feeling entitled to take one. It's not selfish to want to disconnect or say "no" when you're already overwhelmed. On the contrary, it's a sign of self-respect and awareness of your needs.

Surprisingly, social connection also falls under self-care. Humans are social creatures; we need human interactions to feel connected and understood. This can mean spending time with friends or family, joining groups or communities of like-minded individuals, or even seeking professional support during particularly challenging times.

Finally, it's essential to remember that self-care is not a destination but a journey. There is no "right" way to practice self-care; what matters is finding what works for the individual and committing to those practices with intention and mindfulness. The path to self-care is continually evolving, adapting to each person's changing needs along life's journey.

Self-care represents a fundamental component of an individual's overall well-being. It is a concept that encompasses multiple aspects of a person's life and requires constant attention and deep reflection on both physical and emotional needs. First and foremost, self-care should be seen as an investment in oneself. Like any investment, it requires time, resources, and dedication, but the long-term benefits are immeasurable. Self-care should never be regarded as a luxury or indulgence; instead, it is a necessity to maintain balance in today's hectic life.

One of the primary obstacles people face in adopting a consistent self-care practice is guilt. In a society that rewards productivity and constant activity, taking time for oneself can seem like a selfish act. However, it is crucial to understand that taking care of oneself not only benefits the individual but also has positive repercussions for those around them. A person who practices self-care is more likely to have positive energy to share with others, be more patient, understanding, and productive.

Self-care is not a static, one-size-fits-all formula. What works for one person may not work for another. Experimentation and self-reflection are therefore crucial. Listening to your body, mind, and spirit is essential for identifying what you need. This might involve trying different forms of meditation, changing dietary habits, exploring new activities, or simply dedicating more time to rest.

In conclusion, self-care is an ongoing journey of self-discovery and self-affirmation. It is a practice that requires commitment but pays off with a renewed sense of well-being, balance, and satisfaction in life. In a world where individuals are constantly bombarded by external stimuli, expectations, and pressures, self-care emerges as an indispensable compass, guiding individuals toward a more centered, fulfilling life in harmony with themselves.

16. Understanding Forgiveness: Explore what forgiveness truly means and when it is appropriate.

Forgiveness is one of the most debated and complex aspects of the human experience. In many cultures and spiritual traditions, forgiveness is considered an essential virtue, a necessary step toward healing, personal growth, and inner peace. However, its true meaning, implications, and limits are subjects of diverse and sometimes conflicting interpretations. **Nature of Forgiveness:** Forgiveness is not merely the act of "forgetting" a wrong or suppressing feelings of anger or pain. Instead, it is a profound and intentional process through which a person decides to free themselves from the burden of their wounds, acknowledging the pain but choosing not to be defined by it. Forgiveness does not deny the harm suffered but transforms how we perceive and interact with it. **Forgiveness vs. Reconciliation:** It is essential to distinguish between forgiveness and reconciliation. You can forgive someone without necessarily restoring a relationship with them. Reconciliation involves repairing a broken relationship and requires the consent and action of both parties involved. Forgiveness, on the other hand, is a personal choice that can be made independently of the other person's behavior or remorse.

Benefits of Forgiveness: Numerous studies have shown that forgiveness can have psychological and physical benefits. These include reduced stress, anxiety, and depression, improved sleep quality, and a decreased risk of heart problems. Emotionally, forgiveness can lead to greater inner peace and a renewed sense of freedom.

When Is It Appropriate?: Forgiveness should never be forced or rushed. Each individual must determine the right time for themselves. In some cases, particularly in the presence of severe or repeated traumas, the process may take a long time and may require therapeutic support. And in some situations, a person may decide that they cannot or do not want to forgive. This choice is personal and should be respected.

Forgiveness and Oneself: Often, one of the most significant challenges in the forgiveness process is forgiving oneself. Recognizing and accepting one's mistakes, shortcomings, or weaknesses can be painful but is also a crucial step toward personal growth and self-acceptance.

Conclusion: Forgiveness is an intimate and profoundly individual journey. If and when a person chooses to embark on this path, they embark on a process of liberation and genuine understanding. But what is fundamental to remember is that forgiveness is a choice, and every individual has the right to decide when and if it is the right time to do so.

The concept of forgiveness extends beyond the simple notion of "letting go." It delves deeply into the recesses of our psyche and affects how we perceive ourselves, others, and the world around us. Every culture and religious tradition has its interpretation of forgiveness, but some universal themes emerge when exploring this topic in depth.

In many spiritual traditions, forgiveness is seen as a means to achieve a deeper connection with the divine. Holding onto resentment or nurturing feelings of revenge is believed to separate us from the divine or our true selves. This link between forgiveness and spirituality suggests that forgiving is not only an altruistic act towards another individual but also an act of self-healing and self-liberation.

From a psychological perspective, forgiveness can be viewed as a way to overcome trauma.

Many mental health professionals actively encourage individuals to embark on the path of forgiveness as part of their healing journey. However, it is essential to note that forgiveness is not a one-time act but rather a process that may take time and reflection.

It is also crucial to emphasize that forgiveness does not equate to justifying or minimizing the act that caused the pain. One can fully acknowledge the severity of a wrongdoing and, at the same time, choose to forgive. This distinction is crucial because many people mistakenly believe that forgiveness means "forgetting" or "approving" harmful behavior.

In terms of interpersonal relationships, forgiveness can have a significant impact on the dynamics of a relationship. It can create space for reconciliation or, in some cases, a peaceful separation. When you forgive someone, you also release a certain energy that was previously tied to resentment or anger. This release can lead to greater clarity and understanding in future interactions.

However, it is also possible for some individuals to use the concept of forgiveness as a means to manipulate or control others. Statements like "You should forgive me" or "If you were truly spiritual, you would forgive" are examples of how forgiveness can be distorted to serve selfish goals.

It is crucial for each individual to listen to their own intuition and discernment when it comes to deciding when and how to forgive.

Another nuance of forgiveness concerns the distinction between forgiving and trusting again. You can choose to forgive someone for a past wrong, but it does not automatically mean that you must re-establish the same level of trust that existed before. Trust, once broken, may require time and concrete actions to rebuild.

At its core, forgiveness is about liberation. Freeing oneself from the burden of resentment, the grip of revenge, and the shadow of injustice. While one might think that forgiveness primarily benefits the person who caused the harm, in reality, the primary beneficiary of forgiveness is often the one who forgives.

Neuroscience has begun to delve into the depths of forgiveness, seeking to understand how it affects the brain and the body. Some research indicates that harboring resentment can actually impact our physical health, leading to increased stress, high blood pressure, and other related issues. In contrast, forgiveness can promote reduced stress, improved heart health, and potentially increased longevity.

One of the primary challenges of forgiveness is the internal battle between the desire for justice and the willingness to free oneself from emotional burdens. Society often values the idea of "settling the score," and popular culture is full of stories of revenge and justice. These narratives can make it even more challenging to embrace the concept of forgiveness, especially when the wound is deep and personal.

However, it is important to emphasize that forgiveness does not mean giving up on justice. If someone has been wronged, they have the right to seek justice through appropriate means. Forgiveness is more about our inner state and emotional peace than the external action of accepting or rejecting a person or action.

Self-Forgiveness: Navigating an Even More Complex Terrain

There's also the concept of self-forgiveness, which can be even more challenging to navigate. The mistakes we've made, especially those that have caused pain to others, can lead to deep emotional scars. Self-forgiveness requires deep introspection, acceptance, and the willingness to change and grow. The journey toward self-forgiveness might involve confronting old wounds, acknowledging one's own mistakes, and, most importantly, accepting that you are worthy of love and compassion despite imperfections. Often, seeking the guidance of professionals such as therapists or counselors can be helpful in navigating this complex emotional terrain. Moreover, forgiveness is not a monolithic experience; there are various degrees and depths. You might easily forgive a minor offense, while a severe breach of trust could take years to process and forgive. The key is recognizing that each individual has their own pace, and the forgiveness process cannot be rushed. Respect for your emotional journey and acknowledgment of your resilience and healing capacity are crucial on this journey.

The Complex Landscape of Forgiveness
The concept of forgiveness is one of the most complex and multifaceted themes in the human emotional landscape. At its core, it is an act of liberation and compassion, not only for others but crucially for ourselves. It's a release from the burdensome chain of resentment, the erosion of anger, and the weight of vengeance. But as altruistic as it may seem, forgiveness offers tangible benefits to the forgiver rather than the forgiven. From a psychological perspective, harboring grudges and hostilities can have a detrimental impact on our mental health, causing anxiety, stress, and depression. The weight of these unresolved feelings can also manifest physically, leading to muscle tension, insomnia, and other stress-related disorders. In contrast,

forgiveness can provide a sense of peace and liberation, reducing these negative effects on our physical and mental health.

However, the path to forgiveness is rarely linear or simple. Forgiving does not mean forgetting, nor does it necessarily mean reconciling with those who have hurt us. It can simply mean accepting what has happened, letting go of the desire for revenge or punishment. In some cases, it may also involve recognizing that those who have caused harm may have been victims of circumstances or past traumas.

Self-forgiveness, as we've discussed, is a challenge in its own right. Confronting one's mistakes, acknowledging one's role in past conflicts, and accepting that, despite imperfections, you are worthy of love and compassion, is a journey that requires courage and introspection. Many people may find that while they can easily forgive others, self-forgiveness is a much tougher mountain to climb.

In conclusion, forgiveness, whether toward others or oneself, is a deeply personal and individual process. There is no one-size-fits-all solution or a defined roadmap. What is crucial is an awareness of your capacity for healing, an understanding of your resilience, and the willingness to move toward a future where the weight of the past does not define the potential of tomorrow. Forgiveness, in all its forms, is a testament to human strength and the ability to find peace, compassion, and renewal even in the most adverse circumstances.

16. Support Network: The Importance of Understanding and Having a Solid Support System

A support network is a fundamental pillar in an individual's healing and growth process. It consists of a group of people, which may include friends, family, partners, colleagues, or support groups, who offer listening, understanding, and assistance in various ways. Here's an in-depth look at the importance of having a robust support network.

Emotional Validation: One of the key advantages of having a support system in place is that they can validate your feelings. This means they can confirm that what you feel is real, valid, and understandable. This validation can reduce isolation and the feeling that no one can understand what you're going through.

Sharing Experiences: In addition to validation, sharing your experiences with others can provide valuable perspective. Often, discovering that someone has faced similar challenges and found ways to overcome them can be extremely encouraging.

Active Listening: A support network often offers a compassionate ear, ready to listen without judgment. This type of listening, where the individual feels seen and heard, can have a therapeutic effect.

Practical Support: In addition to emotional support, a support network can provide practical assistance. This may include help with specific tasks, advice on useful resources, or simply offering a helping hand when needed.

Positive Reinforcement: While facing challenges, a support network can serve as a reminder of your strengths and abilities. Words of encouragement or small gestures of affection can do much to boost self-esteem and self-confidence.

Outlet for Venting: There are times when pressure becomes overwhelming, and you need an outlet. Having trusted individuals to talk to can provide a safe release for these feelings, preventing potential negative reactions.

Navigating Difficult Decisions: Life often presents complex decisions. Having a group of people to discuss options, weigh pros and cons, can help in making more considered decisions.

Growth through Reflection: Interacting with others can often serve as a mirror, reflecting parts of ourselves that we might not see. This reflection can be essential for personal growth.

Reducing the Sense of Isolation: One of the main challenges in dealing with difficulties, especially with emotionally immature parents, is the feeling of being alone. A support network actively reduces this feeling, providing a sense of community and belonging.

In conclusion, a support network plays a crucial role in an individual's overall well-being, offering a mix of emotional, practical, and psychological support. Regardless of the nature of the challenge or trauma, having a supportive community can make the difference between feeling isolated and overwhelmed and feeling supported and capable of overcoming adversity.

Expanding the Concept of Support

In the context of healing and personal well-being, the support network extends well beyond the traditional concept of friendship or family. Modern society has seen the emergence of various forms of support that can contribute to a more holistic and multidimensional healing experience.

Online Connections: With the rise of social media and online platforms, there are now virtual communities dedicated to support. These platforms can connect individuals from around the world who share similar experiences, allowing for sharing and support that transcends geographical boundaries. Being able to connect with someone on the other side of the world but who shares a similar challenge can be incredibly powerful.

Self-Help Groups: Beyond digital connections, there are physical self-help groups that meet regularly. These groups can be specific to particular challenges or traumas, such as abuse, addiction, or mental health challenges. In these environments, people can share their stories, learn from each other, and build strong mutual support bonds.

Events and Workshops: There are events, seminars, and workshops designed to help people navigate specific life challenges. These events, in addition to providing information and tools, also create opportunities for individuals to connect with others who share similar challenges.

Group Therapeutic Activities: Activities like group therapy, group meditation, or yoga classes can serve as a support network. These sessions not only offer healing tools but also create a sense of community among participants.

Support through Art and Culture: Music, literature, cinema, and other art forms can act as an indirect support network. Through these expressions, people can feel an emotional connection, feel that their experiences are represented, and that they are not alone in their challenges.

Volunteering and Service: Helping others can be a powerful form of healing. Many people discover that by becoming volunteers and supporting others, they can find a sense of purpose and community. This can create a network of mutual support, where you both give and receive at the same time.

Animal Support: Animals, especially pets, can offer a unique type of support. The unconditional love and affection that an animal can provide often serve as an important source of comfort and can act as a buffer against loneliness.

Professional Support: In addition to personal relationships and community connections, it's essential to recognize the importance of professionals such as therapists, counselors, and life coaches. They can provide tools, resources, and safe spaces to work through trauma and challenges.

By incorporating a combination of these resources and connections, an individual can create a robust and resilient support network that can sustain them through life's challenges. The key is to acknowledge that each person needs a different type of support, and what works for one may not work for another. Customizing and continually adapting your support network based on your needs is essential for an effective and sustainable healing journey.

Within the landscape of human relationships, there's a constant need to feel understood, supported, and accepted. That's why a well-structured support network is fundamental to our mental and emotional health. Let's further explore the concept of a support network:

Education and Training: Courses, seminars, and workshops can not only educate but also act as places where people can meet others with similar issues or related goals. Sharing experiences in a learning environment can create a bond of mutual support among participants.

Sports and Recreational Activities: Sports teams, hiking clubs, or other physical activities are excellent for building support networks. When people come together for a common goal, like winning a game or climbing a mountain, deep bonds are formed.

Religious and Spiritual Groups: Many people find support in their religious or spiritual communities. These groups often provide a safe place to share concerns, doubts, and successes, offering a deep spiritual and human connection.

Specialized Online Support: There are forums and online groups dedicated to specific challenges such as anxiety, depression, substance abuse, or specific illnesses. These virtual spaces allow people to connect anonymously, share their stories, and receive advice from those who have had similar experiences.

Self-Care Support Groups: Self-care has become a crucial part of mental health, and there are many groups dedicated to self-care practices like meditation, reflective writing, and art therapy.

Community Events: Participating in local events like fairs, markets, or festivals can help create a sense of belonging to a community. These events can also offer opportunities to learn about local resources and connect with other people in the area.

Retreats and Getaways: There are specific retreats designed to help people disconnect, relax, and reflect. During these retreats, lasting bonds can form with other participants, creating an extended support network.

Interest-Based Groups: Whether it's a book club, gardening group, or photography team, coming together around a common interest can lead to deep and meaningful connections among members.

Every individual needs a personalized combination of these sources of support. The diversity of these networks means that while some may find support in a religious group, others may find it in a sports club or an online forum. What's essential is recognizing the importance of having a network and making efforts to build and maintain it over time. Such networks not only provide immediate support in tough times but also opportunities for growth, learning, and enrichment in everyday life.

Building and maintaining a strong support network is fundamental to an individual's mental health and well-being, especially for those who have faced the challenges of having emotionally immature parents. A support network goes far beyond simply having someone to talk to. It is a complex system of relationships and resources that provides comfort, guidance, encouragement, and even opportunities for personal growth. **Many studies have shown that having a strong support network can help reduce stress levels, improve the ability to face life's challenges, and increase the sense of belonging and purpose.** In particular, when dealing with childhood traumas or challenges, the ability to share and process these experiences with understanding individuals can expedite the healing process.

However, building a support network requires effort. It's not just about seeking help when in crisis but about establishing and nurturing relationships over time. This might mean actively participating in groups, taking the initiative to share personal experiences, or even assisting others in their challenges, recognizing that giving and receiving support are two sides of the same coin.

It's also essential to recognize that not every relationship or group will be beneficial or suitable for every individual. Sometimes, a relationship or group may no longer feel constructive or may become toxic. In these cases, it's crucial to have the awareness and courage to step away and seek other sources of support.

In conclusion, a support network is not a luxury but a necessity. It is a crucial component of every individual's journey toward healing and self-discovery. It offers a compass when feeling lost, comfort during challenging times, and celebration in moments of joy. Every individual deserves a strong and loving support network, and it is an investment that pays off with significant dividends in terms of well-being and happiness.

17. Impact on Personal Relationships: How these experiences affect adult relationships, including partners and children.
Childhood experiences, especially those related to emotionally immature parents, can have significant repercussions on adult relationships, influencing aspects such as trust, communication, vulnerability, and the ability to form meaningful bonds. Let's now delve into how these experiences can manifest in adult relationships.

Trust: One of the cornerstones of healthy relationships is mutual trust. However, for those who grew up in environments where trust was compromised or betrayed, building or maintaining trust in adult relationships can be challenging. The fear of being hurt again can lead to doubting others' intentions or misinterpreting others' actions as threats.

Attachment: Attachment theories suggest that attachment patterns formed in childhood influence adult relationships. Individuals with a tumultuous childhood may develop anxious or avoidant attachment styles, which can manifest as either excessive dependence or excessive emotional distance in adult relationships.

Communication: The ability to communicate openly and effectively is crucial in relationships. Those who had emotionally immature parents might not have had the opportunity to learn healthy communication skills. This can result in difficulties in conveying thoughts and emotions or in handling conflicts constructively.

Vulnerability: Being vulnerable and open with a partner is essential for deep connection. However, if vulnerability was exploited or punished in the past, adults may avoid showing vulnerability, limiting the depth and intimacy of the relationship.

Repetition of Patterns: It is common for adults to unconsciously replicate their parents' behavior patterns in their own relationships. This can manifest through adopting roles similar to those of their parents or choosing partners who reflect their parents' characteristics.

Relationships with Children: Childhood experiences can also influence one's ability to be a parent. The fear of repeating their parents' mistakes or the desire to compensate for their own past deficiencies can affect parenting styles and behaviors.

In conclusion, adult relationships are deeply influenced by childhood experiences. However, with awareness, support, and therapy, it is possible to recognize these patterns, work to modify them, and build healthier and more satisfying relationships.

Emotional Dependency: Individuals who grew up with emotionally immature parents may develop emotional dependency on their partners. This dependency arises from a deep and often unrecognized desire to seek in others what they did not receive in childhood. They seek a partner who can "heal" past wounds and provide the security and acceptance they lacked in their youth. This can lead to imbalanced relationships, where one party feels overly responsible for the other.

Fear of Abandonment: Wounds stemming from emotionally distant or inconsistent parents can instill a profound fear of abandonment. This fear can manifest in various ways in adult relationships, such as being overly clingy, jealousy, or a constant need for reassurance. Self-Esteem: Self-perception is often influenced by how individuals were treated by their parents. If an individual did not feel valued or loved during childhood, they may struggle to perceive themselves as worthy of love or respect in adult relationships. This low self-esteem can lead to tolerating harmful behaviors or entering relationships where their needs are not met.

Difficulty in Conflict Management: The lack of healthy conflict resolution models in the family can result in difficulties in handling disagreements in adult relationships. The individual might tend to either avoid conflicts altogether by withdrawing or suppressing their emotions or react excessively aggressively or defensively in tense situations.

Seeking Approval: Another significant aspect is the constant pursuit of approval. Growing up with emotionally immature parents can lead to a constant need for validation and approval from others, especially romantic partners. This need can become suffocating for the partner and create imbalanced dynamics within the relationship.

Fear of Intimacy: Despite a deep desire for connection, those who had emotionally immature parents may fear true intimacy. This fear stems from the dread of being truly known and, subsequently, rejected or abandoned. Therefore, while having relationships, they may maintain a certain emotional distance, protecting themselves from further hurt.

Recreation of Family Dynamics: Often, individuals unconsciously seek partners who recreate the family dynamics they experienced in childhood. For example, if a parent was critical or domineering, they may find partners with similar traits, in an unconscious attempt to "resolve" past issues.

These are just some of the ways childhood experiences can influence adult relationships. Understanding and being aware of these dynamics is the first step in building healthier and more satisfying relationships.

Parenthood and Motherhood: Those who grew up with emotionally immature parents may not have had an adequate role model on how to be parents themselves. This can manifest in various ways when they become parents. Some may become excessively protective, trying to compensate for what they lost during their own childhood, while others may repeat the same behaviors of their parents, never having learned alternative behavior patterns. The challenge lies in identifying these behaviors and trying to break the cycle.

External Validation Dependency: The lack of recognition and affection from parents can lead to excessive dependency on external validation. This can manifest in relationships where the individual constantly seeks confirmation, compliments, or reassurance from their partner, often to the point of basing their self-worth on the judgment of others.

Emotional Isolation: Some of those who grew up with emotionally immature parents may develop defense mechanisms that lead them to emotionally isolate themselves. Although they may appear sociable and functioning externally, internally, they may maintain a distance, avoiding sharing their true feelings or vulnerabilities.

Difficulty Expressing Emotions: Growing up in an environment where emotions were not accepted or were rejected can lead to difficulties in expressing or recognizing one's own emotions. This can result in superficial communication in relationships or difficulties in understanding and responding to the emotional needs of the partner.

Overadaptation: Sometimes, to cope with emotionally immature parents, a child may become "the little adult" in the family, taking on responsibilities beyond their age. This role can persist into adulthood, causing the individual to overadapt to others' needs, often at the expense of their own needs and desires.

Excessive Self-Criticism: Another side effect of having emotionally immature parents can be the development of excessive self-criticism. Without proper support or recognition in childhood, the individual may internalize criticism and become their harshest judge, questioning every decision or action and feeling that they are never doing enough.

Conflict Avoidance: If conflict was handled poorly in the family, the individual may fear or avoid any form of confrontation in their relationships. This can lead to not addressing significant issues, accumulating resentments or frustrations over time.

The profound impact of childhood experiences on our adult relationships cannot be underestimated. When an individual grows up in an environment characterized by emotionally immature parents, their relational abilities, self-perception, and emotional management can be deeply influenced, often in ways they may not fully recognize until much later in life.

To begin with, how we perceive and interpret love, affection, and security is often rooted in early interactions with our parents or caregivers. If these early relationships are distorted by a lack of empathy, understanding, or support, it is likely that an individual will develop insecure attachment patterns. These patterns can manifest as attachment anxiety, avoidance, or a combination of both, influencing how the individual approaches and responds to intimate relationships.

Furthermore, our sense of self-esteem and self-worth is often a reflection of how we were treated as children. If a child grew up feeling inadequate, unloved, or constantly criticized, these emotional wounds can lead to a distorted self-image. The individual may constantly feel the need for external validation or, conversely, build emotional walls, avoiding intimacy due to fear of rejection or pain.

Partnerships, in turn, can be undermined by these unresolved traumas. Without awareness or understanding of these dynamics, an individual may unconsciously replicate the same behavioral patterns as their parents, perpetuating the cycle of emotional detachment, lack of communication, and potential conflict.

And it's not just romantic relationships that are affected. Relationships with one's children can mirror, in a specular way, the same deficiencies or dynamics experienced in their own childhood. This risks passing on the same insecurities and traumas to the next generation.

In conclusion, addressing and recognizing the impact of one's childhood experiences on adult relationships is crucial not only

for the individual's mental and emotional health but also for the well-being of their future relationships and loved ones. Only through deep reflection, awareness, and in many cases, professional support, can one hope to break the cycle and establish healthier, authentic, and fulfilling relationships.

18. Generational Awareness: Reflect on how to break the cycle to ensure that future generations do not perpetuate the same pattern.

Generational awareness is a profoundly relevant concept when considering the transmission of behavioral patterns, attitudes, and traumas from one generation to the next. Often, individuals inherit not only genetic traits but also emotional, psychological, and behavioral traits from their ancestors. The ability to recognize and break these cycles is essential to ensure healthy and thriving generations in the future.

1. Recognition and Reflection: The first step in breaking any cycle is to acknowledge it. Individuals must become aware of the patterns that manifest in their lives and trace their origins. Keeping a journal, talking to older family members, or even seeking therapy can be

helpful in identifying and understanding these tendencies.

2. Emotional Literacy: Emotional literacy, the ability to recognize, understand, and express one's emotions, is crucial. Emotional education can help individuals navigate their reactions and behaviors, allowing for greater self-understanding.

3. Therapy and Counseling: A professional can provide the tools and strategies needed to address and resolve deep-rooted traumas and behavioral patterns. This may include cognitive-behavioral therapy, family therapy, or other forms of intervention.

4. Open Communication: Talking to one's children or other family members about recognized patterns can help prevent their perpetuation. Shared awareness can serve as an early warning system, helping future generations recognize and avoid certain behaviors.

5. Meditation and Mindfulness: These practices can help center the mind, develop greater self-awareness, and break automatic or impulsive reactions rooted in the past.

6. Parental Education: Attending parenting classes or reading parenting

materials can provide new perspectives and strategies for addressing challenges and avoiding repeating the mistakes of one's parents.

7. Commitment to Personal Growth: In addition to therapy, there are many activities such as reading, workshops, and seminars that can support personal growth and help develop greater self-awareness.

In conclusion, breaking generational cycles of trauma, behaviors, and attitudes requires active and deliberate commitment. It is a journey that may take time, but the benefits of a healthier, happier, and more conscious life, not only for oneself but also for future generations, are invaluable. Through awareness, education, and active engagement in personal growth, it is possible not only to recognize and understand inherited patterns but also to take concrete steps to ensure they are not passed on.

Generational awareness is not just an understanding of behavioral patterns transmitted within a family or community, but it is also a deep introspection into the cultural, historical, and social roots that influence such patterns. For decades, scholars have explored how previous generations can impact the present and how these influences can be altered or interrupted for the benefit of future generations. **In the context of families, oral histories and narratives play a fundamental role in shaping young people's perception of the world.** For example, a grandfather who lived through a war may pass on stories of survival, resilience, and loss to his grandchildren. While these stories can instill values such as resilience and perseverance, they can also carry hidden traumas, fears, and anxieties.

Generational influences do not stop at family stories. The music, art, and literature of a particular era can reflect the emotions and feelings of that generation and inadvertently influence future generations. For example, the folk music of the 1960s, with its themes of protest and social change, had a significant impact on the baby boomer generation and how they perceived activism and social justice.

Economic and political trends also play a key role. The Great Depression of the 1930s created a generation of frugal, savings-oriented individuals who were risk-averse. These economic trends profoundly influenced how this generation educated their children in terms of financial values.

Technology is another key factor. The generation that grew up in a pre-internet era has a completely different view of privacy, communication, and social interaction compared to digital natives. These technological differences inevitably create gaps in understanding and communication between generations. Furthermore, there are psychological and behavioral aspects. For example, a mother who experienced abandonment at a young age may, unknowingly, smother or be excessively protective of her own children, trying to compensate for the trauma she experienced. Or a father who grew up in an environment where showing emotions was considered a sign of weakness might inadvertently instill the same value in his children.

1. **To break these cycles, it is essential for individuals to understand and reflect on these multidimensional factors. The key is not only to recognize and accept these influences but also to actively question how they can be modified or redirected to ensure a better future. Awareness is just the beginning; it is intentional action, dialogue, and openness to growth and change that will lead to real generational change.**

2. **Generational awareness is a concept deeply intertwined with the fabric of the socio-cultural tapestry of a society.** It represents a lens through which we can examine the accumulation of experiences, values, beliefs, and traumas that are passed from one generation to another and often manifest in specific behaviors and attitudes. The key to successfully navigating the complex landscape of generational awareness is first understanding its roots and mechanisms.

3. **To begin with, each generation grows up in a unique historical, political, economic, and social context. This context shapes their collective experiences, which, in turn, influence their mindset and behavior. For example, those who grew up during World War II in Europe will have a very different set of experiences and values from those who grew up in the 1980s in America. These collective experiences form a "generational imprint" that influences how an individual sees and interacts with the world.**

4. **In addition to historical and social experiences, family dynamics play a crucial role in the transmission of certain behaviors and beliefs.** For example, families where open communication is discouraged may

pass on generations of individuals who struggle to express their feelings or confront conflicts in a healthy manner. Or in families where academic or professional performance is strongly emphasized, generations of success-oriented individuals may emerge, potentially at the expense of their mental health or emotional well-being.

5. **The importance of generational awareness lies in its ability to illuminate the inherent and often invisible patterns that guide our behavior. Once these patterns are recognized, individuals and communities have the opportunity to break harmful or unhealthy cycles. Self-reflection, education, and openness to intergenerational dialogue are essential tools in this process.**

6. **Breaking these cycles requires both individual and collective commitment. On an individual level, this may involve therapy or counseling to address deep-seated traumas or beliefs. On a collective level, it may involve educational programs, community initiatives, or social movements aimed at changing culturally entrenched attitudes or challenging social norms.**

7. In conclusion, generational awareness is a powerful lens through which we can examine and understand the profound influences that shape our behavior and beliefs. By recognizing and addressing these influences, we have the opportunity to forge a future where subsequent generations are not bound by the limitations or traumas of the past but are instead equipped with the tools and wisdom to create a healthier and more harmonious future.

19. Recommended Resources and Readings: Provide further materials and resources for those who wish to delve deeper.

1. Books:

"Adult Children of Emotionally Immature Parents" by Lindsay C. Gibson: This book offers a detailed perspective on the dynamics that can emerge between emotionally immature parents and their children, suggesting strategies for managing and overcoming these challenges.

"The Drama of the Gifted Child" by Alice Miller: An in-depth analysis of childhood trauma and its long-term implications.

"The Body Keeps the Score" by Bessel van der Kolk: Explores how physical and emotional trauma can leave a mark on the body and psyche and suggests approaches for healing.

2. Organizations and Support Groups:

8. **Adult Children of Emotionally Immature Parents:** Local and online support groups that provide a listening and sharing space for those who have grown up with emotionally distant or narcissistic parents.

9. **Association for Research and Treatment of Trauma (ARTT):** Offers resources, training, and support for professionals and individuals interested in better understanding trauma and its consequences.

10. **Siti Web e Blog**:
    - **The Invisible Scar**: Un blog focalizzato sul trauma emotivo derivante dall'abuso verbale e psicologico.
    - **Out of the Fog**: Una risorsa online per persone che vivono con familiari affetti da disturbi di personalità. Offre terminologia, strategie e una comunità di supporto.

11. **Corsi e Webinar**:

- **Coursera & Udemy**: Molti corsi online sono disponibili su temi come il trauma, la consapevolezza, la psicologia infantile e le relazioni familiari. Questi possono offrire approfondimenti e strategie pratiche.

12. **Podcast**:
    - **The Mental Illness Happy Hour**: Anche se copre una vasta gamma di argomenti legati alla salute mentale, molti episodi affrontano il tema del trauma infantile e delle relazioni familiari tossiche.
    - **Therapy Chat**: Questo podcast ospita vari esperti che discutono di trauma, attaccamento e guarigione.

13. **Articoli e Journals**:
    - **Google Scholar**: Una ricerca su "emotional immaturity", "childhood trauma", o "parent-child relationships" può portare a numerosi articoli scientifici e studi rilevanti sul tema.

These resources represent only a small fraction of what is available. It is advisable to consult with a mental health professional or librarian for further recommendations tailored to individual needs. Ongoing research, education, and

support are essential for those seeking to understand and heal from challenges related to emotionally immature parents. Understanding and navigating childhood characterized by emotionally immature parents is a holistic journey. Here are some additional resources and suggestions:

7. Documentaries and Films:

- Many films and documentaries explore the complexity of toxic family dynamics and the impact of childhood trauma. Watching these portrayals can offer insights for reflection and give a voice to experiences that may otherwise be difficult to articulate. Titles such as "Running from Crazy" and "The Glass Castle" can be particularly enlightening.

8. Apps and Digital Tools:

- **Headspace and Calm:** Although primarily known as meditation tools, these apps offer specific sessions on pain, trauma, and stress management.

- **BetterHelp and Talkspace:** Online therapy platforms that connect individuals with professionals from around the world, ensuring accessibility and confidentiality.

9. Workshops and Retreats:

- There are many retreats and workshops focused on healing from trauma, personal empowerment, and intuition development. These events can provide tools and practices to deepen self-understanding and initiate the healing process.

10. Music and Art:

- Art has the power to heal, and many people find solace in listening to music or engaging in visual art that reflects their experiences. Creating personalized playlists or dedicating time to painting, writing, or dancing can provide a way to process and express emotions.

11. Local Resources:

- Many community or university centers offer seminars, courses, and support groups on topics related to trauma, childhood, and mental health. These are also places where one can connect with others who share similar experiences.

12. Self-Help Groups:

- In addition to specific groups for adults with emotionally immature parents, there are many other support groups focused on trauma, abuse, and personal growth. These groups can offer a sense of community and belonging.

13. Yoga and Mind-Body Techniques:

- Practices such as yoga, tai chi, and qigong can help reconnect with the body and manage stress. Many studies have shown that these practices can be particularly beneficial for those who have experienced trauma.

14. Conferences and Events:

- Attending conferences on psychology, trauma, and healing can provide new perspectives and approaches. These events can also offer networking opportunities and connections with experts in the field.

  Exploring a combination of these resources, individuals can find what resonates best for them and build a healing journey that is unique and meaningful.

  Of course, delving into recommended resources and readings is key to helping individuals access valuable and educational tools.

Let's continue with further considerations:

15. Podcasts and Radio Programs:

- The audio format can be particularly useful for those on the go or who prefer listening over reading. There are numerous podcasts dedicated to trauma, psychology, and relationships. Listening to others' experiences can offer comfort, recognition, and new perspectives. Some examples include "The Trauma Therapist Podcast," "Where Should We Begin? with Esther Perel," and "Mental Illness Happy Hour."

16. Games and Simulations:

- With the growing popularity of therapeutic games and simulations, there are now interactive platforms that can help individuals explore and work on complex themes such as relationships, trauma, and self-awareness. These tools can offer a different and engaging mode of reflection and introspection.

17. Bibliotherapy:

- Bibliotherapy, the use of books as a therapeutic tool, can be an effective strategy. Not only self-help books or essays but also novels and poetry can provide profound insights and comfort. Readings like "The Language of the Body" by Alexander Lowen or "Narcissism and Relationships" by Wendy T. Behary can offer valuable food for thought.

18. Academic Journals:

- For those inclined toward research and seeking a deeper understanding based on scientific studies, there are many academic journals publishing research on trauma, relationships, and psychology. Access to these journals can provide evidence-based insights and updates on the latest discoveries in the field.

19. Forums and Online Communities:

- In the digital age, online communities such as Reddit, Quora, and other dedicated forums can be valuable resources. Here, individuals can share their stories, seek advice, and receive support from a community of people who have similar experiences. It's essential, however, to ensure navigating safe and moderated spaces.

20. Online Seminars and Webinars:

- Many professionals and organizations offer online seminars on various topics related to mental health and relationships. These can range from free introductory sessions to intensive paid courses.

21. Reading Apps:

- Apps like Audible or Blinkist can provide summaries or audio versions of relevant books, making learning and reflection more accessible for those with limited time or a preference for alternative formats to traditional reading.

22. Newspapers and Magazines:

- Many newspapers and magazines, both in print and digital formats, have sections dedicated to psychology, well-being, and relationships. Articles and interviews can offer fresh and current insights, with a variety of perspectives and voices.

By exploring and combining various resources, individuals can create a personalized path to better understand and navigate the challenges of relationships with emotionally immature parents. The key is curiosity and openness to personal growth.

In conclusion, actively researching and choosing the right resources to address and understand the challenges of relationships with emotionally immature parents are fundamental to the healing and personal understanding process. The variety of available resources reflects the diversity of people's needs and learning methods.

The importance of such resources cannot be emphasized enough. They provide not only information and insights but often offer a sense of belonging and not being alone in one's experience. This sense of recognition and community is vital for many individuals as it enables them to initiate the healing process and see beyond their personal challenges.

However, while access to resources is broader and more varied than ever, it's essential to approach it with a sense of discernment. Not all resources will be equally useful or resonant for every individual. What may work for one person may not be suitable for another. Therefore, it's crucial to listen to oneself, reflect on one's needs, and seek feedback or advice from professionals when necessary.

Furthermore, it's crucial to consider the credibility and reliability of resources. With the abundance of information online, it's easy to come across unverified or potentially harmful advice. Referring to academic sources, certified professionals, and recognized organizations can help ensure the quality of the information received.

Finally, while resources can offer tools, advice, and information, the real work of understanding and healing is intrinsic. This requires time, patience, and often the assistance of mental health professionals. Resources are there to guide, enlighten, and support, but the path of growth and healing remains deeply personal. In summary, recommended resources and readings are an essential complement to the journey of those seeking to understand and address the challenges of relationships with emotionally immature parents. They offer a map, but the journey belongs to the individual. With care, reflection, and commitment, resources can illuminate the path toward greater understanding and well-being.

20. Exercises and Practical Techniques:
- Include exercises, meditations, and techniques to help adults work on their healing.
Exercises and practical techniques can be invaluable tools to help individuals work on their healing, especially those who have faced the challenges of having emotionally immature parents. These activities aim not only to provide immediate relief but also to build long-term skills and strategies for managing emotions and promoting personal growth.

1. Reflective Journaling:

- Writing can be a powerful form of self-exploration. Dedicating 10-15 minutes each day to freely write about one's thoughts, feelings, and reactions can offer valuable insights into one's experiences.

2. Mindfulness Meditation:

- This practice encourages individuals to focus on the present, accepting their thoughts and feelings without judgment. It can help reduce anxiety and build greater self-awareness.

3. Guided Visualization:

- Through this technique, individuals can imagine a safe place or a positive experience, which can offer temporary relief from stressful or overwhelming feelings.

4. Diaphragmatic Breathing:

- Focusing on deep, controlled breathing can calm the nervous system and help manage anxiety and stress.

5. Grounding Exercises:

- These exercises help connect with the present, especially during moments of dissociation or acute stress. For example, listing five things you can see, four things you can touch, three things you can hear, two things you can smell, and one thing you can taste.

6. Positive Affirmations:

- Creating a list of positive and reassuring affirmations can be helpful. Reading them aloud or reciting them daily can strengthen self-esteem and self-confidence.

7. Gratitude Practice:

- Keeping a gratitude journal and jotting down three things to be grateful for each day can shift the focus from negative experiences to positive ones.

8. Muscle Relaxation Techniques:

- This involves tensing and relaxing specific muscle groups, helping release physical tension and promote calm.

9. Grounding Techniques:

- Walking barefoot on grass, hugging a tree, or simply sitting on the earth can help feel connected and grounded.

10. Active Listening Exercises:

- Practicing active listening with a partner or friend can help improve communication skills and build deeper and more meaningful relationships.

In conclusion, these practical techniques and exercises offer individuals tangible tools to begin and support their healing journey. While some techniques may resonate more than others, the important thing is to find what works best for the individual and integrate it into their daily

routine. With commitment and regular practice, these exercises can support and nurture inner growth and healing. Absolutely, let's further explore other techniques and approaches that can be used to support personal healing:

11. Yoga and Body Movement:

- The physical act of moving can release accumulated tension and restore a sense of balance in the body. Yoga, in particular, integrates the mind, body, and spirit and is recognized for promoting self-awareness and self-acceptance.

12. Art Therapy:

- Expressing oneself through art—whether drawing, painting, sculpting, or any other artistic form—can provide a way to process and release repressed emotions. You don't need to be an "artist" to benefit from art therapy.

13. Animal Therapy:

- Pets, such as dogs and cats, can offer immediate comfort. Interacting with animals can lower cortisol levels (the stress hormone) and increase oxytocin, promoting feelings of happiness and trust.

14. Time Management:

- Building a daily routine can help establish a sense of normalcy and control. This can include scheduling regular periods for relaxation techniques, physical exercise, time with friends, or any activities that bring joy.

15. Music Therapy:

- Listening to or creating music can have a profound effect on our emotional well-being. Music can evoke emotions, help process feelings, or simply offer an escape.

16. Nature Therapy:

- Spending time in nature, such as walks in the woods, gardening, or simply being outdoors, can have healing effects. Connecting with the earth and the natural environment can be deeply rejuvenating.

17. Assertiveness Exercises:

- Practicing assertiveness can help establish healthy boundaries and express needs and desires effectively.

18. Role-Playing:

- This can be done with a therapist or a trusted friend. Revisiting or recreating challenging situations through role-play can help see things from a different perspective and develop new coping strategies.

19. Culinary Mindfulness:

- The act of cooking and eating mindfully can be a meditative exercise. Focusing on the flavors, smells, and textures of food can be a way to anchor oneself in the present moment.

20. Bibliotherapy:

- Reading can offer insights and comfort. Whether it's fiction or non-fiction works, immersing oneself in a book can provide new perspectives or simply offer a moment of escape.
  The above-mentioned techniques are just some of the many strategies available. Each individual is unique, and what works for one person may not be effective for another. The key is to experiment with different techniques to discover what resonates and helps in one's healing journey.

Approach to Self-Healing and Managing Childhood Wounds from Emotionally Immature Parents:

- The approach to self-healing and managing wounds stemming from childhood with emotionally immature parents is a complex and highly individual journey. The wide range of techniques and tools available reflects the diversity of personal experiences and needs.
  The exercises and techniques mentioned earlier are potentially powerful tools that can help individuals reconnect with themselves, process past traumas, and build a healthier and more integrated future. However, it's essential to

emphasize that not all tools will be effective for everyone, and the process of identifying the most appropriate techniques may take time, experimentation, and often, the guidance of a professional.
The key to healing doesn't solely lie in adopting specific techniques but in the approach taken on this journey:

1. **Self-Awareness:**
   - A deep understanding of oneself is fundamental. Recognizing one's feelings, fears, desires, and needs allows for the healing process to begin from a position of strength.

2. **Patience and Kindness Toward Oneself:**
   - Healing doesn't happen overnight. There may be a need to confront difficult moments, intense feelings, and painful memories. Treating oneself with kindness and compassion during these times is vital.

3. **Seeking Support:**
   - While exercises can be practiced individually, having the support of therapists, support groups, or trusted friends can make a significant difference. Sharing, listening, and the feeling of not being alone in the journey are invaluable resources.

4. **Respecting Personal Limits:**
   - If a technique or exercise feels too overwhelming, it's crucial to listen to oneself and take a step back if necessary.
5. **Consistent Commitment:**
   - Healing is a journey, not a destination. It requires consistent commitment and, at times, the willingness to revisit and work on aspects that may resurface over time.
6. **Evolution and Adaptation:**
   - As one progresses on the journey, needs may change. What works at a particular moment may not be effective later on. Being open to adaptation and experimenting with new tools can be crucial.

In conclusion, while the wound of having emotionally immature parents can have profound and lasting impacts, the capacity for healing and growth exists within every individual. With the right resources, the correct approach, and dedicated commitment, it is possible to navigate this journey successfully and find greater integration, peace, and well-being in one's life.

Conclusion and Book Summary: Emotionally Immature Parents - Navigating and Healing: Living with emotionally immature parents can leave deep imprints on an individual's psyche. This book has explored a wide range of aspects, tools, and techniques to help those who wish to heal and grow.

1. **Introduction to Emotional Immaturity:**
   - Understanding the roots and manifestations of emotional immaturity is the first step in addressing the issue.
2. **Signs and Symptoms:**
   - Recognizing behaviors and reactions associated with these experiences can help identify and process past traumas.
3. **Understanding One's Wounds:**
   - Thoughtful introspection can help better understand how traumas have manifested throughout life.
4. **Trauma Processing:**
   - Through techniques like EMDR and cognitive-behavioral therapy, the healing journey can begin.
5. **Focusing on the Present:**
   - Living in the present helps detach from past pain.
6. **Self-Rediscovery:**
   - Reconnecting with one's essence and passions is fundamental for a fulfilling life.
7. **Establishing Boundaries:**

- Creating protective barriers is essential to ensure emotional well-being.

8. **Managing Anger and Resentment:**
   - Techniques like meditation can help manage and process these feelings.

9. **Rebuilding Relationships:**
   - Creating new dynamics with parents or renegotiating terms can be beneficial.

10. **Therapeutic Support:**
    - Therapy is a fundamental resource in the healing journey.

11. **Case Studies:**
    - Real-life examples can offer inspiration and understanding.

12. **Importance of Self-Care:**
    - Taking care of oneself is crucial for long-term well-being.

13. **Understanding Forgiveness:**
    - Deep reflections on the meaning and importance of forgiveness.

14. **Support Network:**
    - Having a solid network can make a difference in the healing journey.

15. **Impact on Personal Relationships:**
    - Recognizing how past experiences influence current relationships.

16. **Generational Awareness:**
    - The importance of breaking the cycle for future generations.

17. **Resources and Recommended Readings:**
   - Additional tools and readings can deepen the understanding.
18. **Exercises and Practical Techniques:**
   - Practical tools for actively working on one's healing.

Useful Resources and Websites:

- Psychology Today: A website offering a wide range of articles and resources on various psychological topics, along with a list of therapists.
- The International Society for Traumatic Stress Studies: A specialized resource on trauma and PTSD.
- Mind: A UK-based charity dedicated to mental health.
- Books: "Running On Empty" by Dr. Jonice Webb and "Adult Children of Emotionally Immature Parents" by Lindsay C. Gibson.

In conclusion, while the challenges related to having emotionally immature parents are real and profound, the available resources and techniques offer hope and pathways to authentic healing. Every individual has the capacity to navigate this journey, find peace, and build a brighter and more fulfilling future.